INTRODUCTION TO INDIAN ART

Introduction to Indian Art

ANANDA K. COOMARASWAMY

Edited by
MRS ANANDA K. COOMARASWAMY

MANOHAR
2026

First published 1947
Reprinted 2026

ISBN 978-81-19139-07-1 (Hb)
ISBN 978-81-19139-25-5 (Pb)

Published by
Ajay Kumar Jain *for*
Manohar Publishers & Distributors
4753/23 Ansari Road, Daryaganj
New Delhi 110 002

Printed at
Replika Press Pvt. Ltd.

CONTENTS

LIST OF ILLUSTRATIONS

Fig. 40. Śri Rāgiṇī. Late 16th century, Rajput, Rājasthānī. Paper.

Fig. 41. Madhu-mādhavī Rāgiṇī. Early 17th century. Rajput, Rājasthānī.

Fig. 42. Siege of Laṅkā (*Rāmāyaṇa*). Rajput, Pahāṛī. Late 17th century. Paper.

Fig. 43. *Rāmāyaṇa* (Vana-parva). *ca.* 1700 (?). Paper.

Fig. 44. Kṛṣṇa Veṇugopāla. *ca.* 1700 (?) Paper.

ABBREVIATIONS

Archaeological Survey of India, Annual Reports	A.S.I.-A.R.
Journal Asiatique, Paris	J.A.
Memoirs of the Asiatic Society of Bengal	M.A.S.B.
Bulletin de l'Ecole francaise d'Extreme-Orient, Hanoi	B.E.F.E.O.
Bulletin de la Societe Linguistique	Bull. Soc. Ling.
Bulletin of the School of Oriental Studies	B.S.O.S.
Cambridge History of India, Vol. 1, 1922	C.H.I.
Memoirs de la Delegation en Perse	Delegation en Perse
Journal of the Royal Asiatic Society, London	J.R.A.S.
Journal of the Bihar and Orissa Research Society	J.B.O.R.S.
Indian Antiquary	I.A.
Ostasiatische Zeitschrift	O.Z.
Jahrbuch der preussischen Kunstsammlungen, Berlin	Jahrb. d. preuss Kunsts.
Sitzungsberichte Akademie der Wissenschaten, Berlin	Sitz. bai. Ak. Wiss.

INTRODUCTION

'Art in India' and 'art' in the modern world mean two very different things. In India, it is the statement of a racial experience, and serves the purposes of life, like daily bread. Indian art has always been produced in response to a demand: that kind of idealism which would glorify the artist who pursues a personal ideal of beauty and strives to express himself, and suffers or perishes for lack of patronage, would appear to Indian thought far more ridiculous or pitiable than heroic. The modern world, with its glorification of personality, produces works of genius and works of mediocrity following the peculiarities of individual artists: in India, the virtue or defect of any work is the virtue or defect of the race in that age. The names and peculiarities of individual artists, even if we could recover them, would not enlighten us: nothing depends upon genius or requires the knowledge of an individual psychology for its interpretation. To understand at all, we must understand experiences common to all men of the time and place in which a given work was produced. All Indian art has been produced by professional craftsmen following traditions handed down in pupillary succession. Originality and novelty are never intentional. Changes in form, distinguishing the art of one age from that of another, reflect the necessities of current theology and not the invention of genius: changes in quality reflect the varying, but not deliberately varied, changes in racial psychology, vitality and taste. What is new arises constantly in Indian tradition without purpose or calculation on the part of the craftsman, simply because life has remained over long extended periods an immediate experience. Tradition is a living thing, and utterly unlike the copying of styles which has replaced tradition in modern life. No such failure of energy as archaism represents appears in Indian art before the twentieth century.

In India, the same qualities pervade all works of any given period, from pottery to architecture, and all are equally expressive: the smallest fragment of a textile portrays the same as the most elaborate temple. In other words, there are no distinctions of fine and applied or decorative art and no unsurmountable barrier dividing the arts of the folk from the canonical arts. Indian art has always an intelligible meaning and a definite purpose. An 'art for art's sake', a 'fine' or useless art, if it could have been imagined, would only have been regarded as a monstrous product of human vanity. The modern 'fine' or useless arts are unrelated to life and speak in riddles—and hence the utter impossibility of inculcating a 'love of art' in the people at large. A race producing great art, however, does so, not by its 'love of art', but by its love of life. In India, where no one discussed art (there is no Sanskrit equivalent for the modern concept of 'art'), where none but philosophers discussed the theory of beauty, and where sculptures and paintings were regarded not as 'works of art', but as means to definite ends—there, art was an integral quality inhering in all activities, entertained by all in their daily environment, and produced by all in proportion to the vitality (not the kind) of their activity.

INTRODUCTION TO INDIAN ART

CHAPTER ONE

INDO-SUMERIAN

IT has long been known that seals of a type unique in India have been found in the Indus valley.[1] Quite recently excavations at two sites, Harappa in the Panjab and Mohenjo-Daro in Sind, have revealed the existence of extensive city-sites with remains of brick buildings by no means of a primitive character, and an abundance of minor antiquities indicating a period of transition from the stone to the copper age. These remains underlie those of the Kuṣāṇa period, but are not far from the surface; the existence of still lower strata suggests that the Indus valley culture must have had a long previous history in the same area and that it may be regarded as indigenous.[2] "The more we learn of the copper age," says Rostovtzeff, "the more important it is seen to be. This epoch created brilliant centres of cultured life all over the world, especially in the Orient. To the centres already known, Elam, Mesopotamia and Egypt, we can now add Turkestan and Northern Caucasus."[3] And finally the Indus valley. It may be remarked too that the further we go back in history, the nearer we come to a common cultural type; the further we advance, the greater the differentiation. The chalcolithic culture was everywhere characterised by matriarchy and a cult of the productive powers of nature, and of a mother goddess; and by a great development of the arts of design. An early culture of this kind once extended from the

1 Cunningham, *Archaeological Survey Reports*, 1862-1887, vols. I-XXIII, Calcutta, 1871-1887; Fleet, J. F., *Seals from Harappa*, J. R. A. S., 1922.

2 For the Indus valley discoveries, still in progress, see Marshall, *First Light on a Long-forgotten Civilization*, III, London News, Sept. 20, 1924; *Unveiling the Prehistoric Civilization of India*, Illustrated London News, Feb. 27 and March 6, 1926, and A.S.I.-A.R., 1921-22, pl. XIII and 1923-24, pp. 47-54; Chanda, *Beginning of the sikhara of the nagara (Indo-Aryan) Temple, Rūpam*, 17, 1924.

3 *The Iranians and Greeks in South Russia*, Oxford, 1922.

Mediterranean to the Ganges valley, and the whole of the Ancient East has behind it this common inheritance.

The antiquities found in the Indus valley, other than brick buildings and a limited amount of masonry, include limestone figures of bearded men (Fig. 1), and terracottas representing female figures and animals, the latter including the rhinoceros, now extinct in the Indus valley. No anthropomorphic images, other than the terracottas, have been found; but a blue faience tablet with pictographic characters at the back has in front the representations of a cross-legged figure, with kneeling worshippers right and left, and a Nāga behind, a remarkable anticipation of familiar types in later Buddhist art of the historical period. Painted pottery analogous to the prehistoric pottery of Baluchistan is abundant; it may be remarked that in Baluchistan there survives an isolated Dravidian language, Brahui, which had long been regarded as a possible island, connecting Dravidian India with the West. Other remains include beads and ornaments of chank, cornelian, etc.; ring stones or maces; faience bangles; haematite pestles; polished gold jewellery; coins; abundant neolithic implements; and above all, seals. Iron is lacking, and the horse was unknown.

The seals (Figs. 2-6) are of ivory, or blue or white faience, square in form, and with a perforated boss at the back for suspension. They bear a great variety of designs, including bulls both with and without humps, elephants, tigers, and a representation of a *pippala* tree (*Ficus religiosa*) with two horned monsters affronted attached to the stem. Further, the seals bear numerous characters of a pictographic script which it has not yet been possible to decipher.[4] The representation of these various animals, especially that of the bull and elephant, is masterly in the extreme; that of the limestone sculpture is

4 Attempted by Waddell, *Indo-Sumerian Seals Deciphered,* London, 1925, and note in J.R.A.S., Jan. 1926. Waddell identified Sumerians with Aryans; the equation Sumerian = Dravidian is much more plausible. For another attempt to read the seals see Bishan Svarup in J.B.O.R.S., IX, 1923, and criticisms by Chanda in the same volume. Some scholars connect Assyrians with Asuras.

aesthetically decadent, rather than primitive.

It has been shown that these antiquities bear a general resemblance to those found on Sumerian sites in Mesopotamia, especially Kish and Susa, dating from the fifth to third millennium B.C. The resemblance amounts to identity in the case of an early Sumerian glazed steatite seal from Kish, alike in respect to the script and of the bull, but this is evidence of trade relations rather than community of language. The miniature funeral potteries of both areas are almost indistinguishable; it may be noted, too, that the oblong, short-legged terracotta sarcophagi of prehistoric South Indian sites are of Mesopotamian type. Cornelian beads found at Kish are decorated with white lines on a red ground, obtained by local calcination of the surface; this technique, unknown in the west of Mesopotamia, is so common in India, though at a later date, as to suggest a probable Indian origin.[5] Some Indian boat designs are of a Mesopotamian character, the coracle in particular, while the presence of conch at Susa and of teak and Indian cedar in Babylon are evidences of a seaborne trade, as early as the eighth century B.C., nor is there much reason to doubt that it had begun still earlier.[6]

While the remains alluded to above as found in the Sind valley certainly go back to the third or fourth millennium B.C. it must not be supposed that a complete hiatus divides this early period from later times. A part of the remains at Mohenjo-Daro probably dates between 1000 and 400 B.C., and on the other hand the minor antiquities from various Indian sites, as at Basāṛh, Taxila (Bhiṛ mound), Pāṭaliputra, and South Indian prehistoric sites go back at least to the fifth century B.C.

The study of Indo-Sumerian antiquities is still in its infancy, and it is too early to draw far-reaching conclusions. But it is

5 Mackay, E., *Sumerian Connections with Ancient India*, J.R.A.S., 1925; Bloch, Th., *Excavations at Basāṛh*, A.S.I.-A.R., 1903-04. Another seal of the same type was found in the old cemetery at Ur, but has cuneiform text (J.R.A.S., 1927, p. 670).

6 Hornell, J., *The Origins and Ethnological Significance of Indian Boat Designs*, M.A.S.B., VII, 1920.

at least probable "that the civilization of which we have now obtained this first glimpse was developed in the Indus valley itself and was as distinctive of that region as the civilization of the Pharaohs was distinctive of the Nile"; and if the Sumerians, as is generally supposed, represent an intrusive element in Mesopotamia, "then the possibility is clearly suggested of India proving ultimately to be the cradle of their civilization, which in its turn lay at the root of Babylonian, Assyrian and Western Asiatic culture generally."[7]

7 Marshall, A.S.I.-A.R., 1923-24. For the theory of the eastern origin of Western Asiatic and even Egyptian culture, with special reference to the origin of copper and of early religious systems, see de Morgan, J., *La préhistoire orientale,* vols. 1 and 2, Paris, 1925-26. See also Rostovtzeff, *Inlaid Bronzes of the Han Dynasty* (Paris, 1927), p. 5: "new discoveries both in Elam and in India...show that some of the important elements of Sumerian art were not created in Mesopotamia."

CHAPTER TWO

DRAVIDIANS AND ARYANS

CERTAINLY before the second millennium B.C. the Dravidians, whether of western origin, or as seems quite probable, of direct neolithic descent on Indian soil, had come to form the bulk of a population thinly scattered throughout India. These Dravidians should be the Dāsas or Dasyus with whom the conquering Aryans waged their wars; their *purs* or towns, are mentioned in the Vedas, and they are described as *anāsaḥ,* noseless, a clean indication of their racial type.

Amongst the elements of Dravidian origin are probably the cults of the phallus[8] and of mother-goddess, Yakṣas, Nāgas and other nature spirits; and many of the arts. Indeed, if we recognize in the Dravidians a southern race, and in the Aryans a northern, it may well be argued that the victory of kingly over tribal organizations, the gradual reception into orthodox religion of the phallus cult and mother-goddess, and the shift from abstract symbolism to anthropomorphic iconography in the period of theistic and *bhakti* development, mark a final victory of the conquered over the conquerors. In particular, the popular, Dravidian element, must have played the major part in all that concerns the development and office of image-worship, that is *pūjā* as distinct from *yajña.*[9]

8 Worshippers of the *śiśna* are mentioned with disapproval in the Vedas. A prehistoric *lingam* is illustrated by Foote, R.B., *The Foote Collection of Indian Prehistoric and Protohistoric Antiquities,* Madras, 1914; see *Notes on their Age and Distribution,* Madras, 1916, pl. XV; the term itself is non-Aryan (Przyluski, J., *Emprunts anāryens en indo-aryen,* Bull. Soc. Ling., 24, 1924, p. 118; Poussin, de la Vallée, *Indo-Européens et Indo-Iraniens : l'Inde jusque vers* 300 *av. J.C.*, Paris, 1924, p. 199; Charpentier, Jarl, *Über den Begriff und die Etymologie von pūjā,* Festgabe Hermann Jacobi, Bonn, 1926. Objects resembling *lingams* have been found at Mohenjo-Daro.

9 For the theory of northern and southern races see Strzygowski, *Altai-*

To the Dravidians are probably due the forms of architecture based on bamboo construction; the architecture of the Toḍa hut has been cited as a prototype, or at any rate a near analogue, of the early barrel-vaulted *caitya*-hall and horse-shoe arch.[10] Curved roofs, common in India, are rare in the rest of the world. The stone slab construction of many early temples is likewise of Dravidian (dolmen) origin. Early maritime trade and all that has to do with fishing must be Dravidian. The chank or conch industry is a case in point; the use of chank bangles, and of the conch as a trumpet in ritual and war must have been borrowed from Dravidian sources before the epic period.[11]

The early history of the Dravidians in the Deccan and Southern India is obscure. It is fairly evident that in these areas Dravidian culture had already attained a high level, economic, martial and literary, in centuries preceding the Christian era. Already in the third century B.C. the great Āndhra empire stretched across the Deccan from east to west.[12] In the far south a powerful and prosperous Pāṇḍyan kingdom flourished before the beginning of the Christian era, with a capital at Korkai. The first three centuries of the Christian era represent an Augustan period in the history of Tamil culture,

Iran, etc. In India, Marshall, *The Influence of Race on Early Indian Art,* and Kramrisch, *Rūpam,* 18, 1924, pp. 69-76.

10 Simpson, W., *Origin and Mutation in Indian and Eastern Architecture, Indian Architecture,* Trans. Roy. Inst. British Architects, 1891, pp. 225-76. But I cannot regard the "Indo-Āryan" *śikhara* as directly derived from a primitive type of bamboo construction: it is later development, produced by the reduplication of vertically compressed storeys. Cf., these theories are summarised in Chanda, R.P., *Beginning of the sikhara of the nagara (Indo-Aryan) Temple, Rūpam,* 17, 1924, with references.

11 Hornell, J., *The Sacred Conch of India,* Madras, 1914. The conch as a ceremonial object is honoured in *Atharvaveda,* XIX, 22. *Śaṅkha-saṁyutti,* shell garlands decorating architecture, are mentioned in the *Mahāvaṁśa,* XXVII, 16; knife handles, thimbles, and boxes made of *śaṅkha-nābhi* (inner central part terminating in the spiral tip or 'navel') in the *Cullavagga,* V, 11, 1 and 5, and *Mahāvagga,* VI, 12, 1.

12 Smith, V.A., *Early History of India,* 4th ed., Oxford, 1924, p. 217; Jouveau-Dubreuil, *Ancient History of the Deccan,* Pondicherry, 1920; Bhandarkar, Sir R.G., *Early History of the Dekkhan.*

and there is sufficient literary evidence for a high state of development of poetry, music, drama, sculpture and painting. At the same time there had grown up a flourishing trade with Rome on the one hand, and with Farther India and Indonesia on the other, the principal articles of export being pepper, cinnamon, pearls and beryl.[13]

A brief reference must be made to the prehistoric Indian antiquities which cannot be exactly placed or dated. Eoliths have been found in India and Ceylon, and paleoliths are widely distributed. Remains of the Neolithic cultures, some of incalculable age, others later than the beginning of the Christian era, include the usual types of stone weapons, pottery, and dolmens. In northern India a copper age succeeded and in part overlapped (Mohenjo-Daro, etc.) the neolithic. Finds of copper weapons have been made in many places, the most important being that at Gungeria, C.P., where silver ornaments were also found. The weapons include bare and shouldered celts, plain and barbed spearheads, swords and harpoons, often in handsome shapes and finely wrought; some are of great weight and may have been used for cult purposes. There is no bronze age, nor does bronze begin to appear much before the first century A.D. Iron may have come into use in the earlier part of the first millennium B.C., or may have been known to the Aryans still earlier; the facts that there is no copper age in the south, that there is a continuity of stone and iron using cultures, that the technique of chank working requires a thin iron saw[14], and that iron weapons (of uncertain age) are characteristic of prehistoric sites in the south, that iron ore is abundant and readily worked, and that steel was known already in India and Ceylon in the second century B.C., all suggest that iron and steel may have come into use at an early date and may have been discovered in India. [Against this view are the facts that iron is not mentioned in the early Vedic literature, and that the

13 Smith, *Early History of India,* Ch. XVI; Aiyangar, M.D., *Tamil Studies,* Madras, 1914; Kanakasabhai, V., *The Tamils Eighteen Hundred Years Ago,* Madras, 1904.

14 Hornell, *The Sacred Conch of India,* Madras, 1914.

Hittites were using iron already about 1500 B.C. The Khalybes, who were neighbours of the Hittites, and perhaps of the same race, had the reputation of being the discoverers of steel; in any case, they were its transmitters to the Greeks].[15] The existence in India of Muṇḍā languages, of Mon-Khmer affinity, seems to show that the southward migration of Sino-Tibetan races which peopled the Irawadi, Menam and Mekong valleys and the Indonesian islands had also entered India at some very early period. A pre-Dravidian element in Southern India is probably Negrito or proto-Malay, and Hornell finds a trace of this first connection of India with the east in the single outrigger boat. Sylvain Lévi recognizes survivals of a pre-Dravidian language in the occurrence of doublet place-names.[16]

The Aryans, whose origin is uncertain, appear in India and Western Asia about the same time. The Indo-Iranian separation may date about 2500 B.C. Aryan names are recognizable in the

15 For the prehistoric remains see Foote, *loc.cit.*, 1, 2; Bloomfield, A., *Silver and Copper Objects found near the Village of Gungeria (C.P.)*, Proc. A.S.B., 1870; Smith, V.A., in *Imperial Gazetteer*, vol. II; Longhurst, in A.S.I.- A.R., Southern Circle, 1914-15 and references in *Cambridge History of India*, vol. 1, 1922, pp. 692, 693. Most of the literature on the stone age in Ceylon will be found in Spolia Zeylanica (Colombo). For the literature on iron see Bhandarkar, D.R., *Excavations at Besnagar*, A.S.I.- A.R., 1913-14 and 1914-15. For steel manufacture in early and mediaeval India, see Hatfield, Sir R., *Siṅhalese Iron and Steel of Ancient Origin*, in Journ. Iron and Steel Institute, I, London, 1912, and in Proc. Roy. Soc., A., vol. 86, 1912; Lester, I.E., *Indian Iron*, Presidential Address, Staffordshire Iron and Steel Institute, Stourbridge, 1912; Belck, W., *Die Erfinder der Eisentechnik*, Zt. für Ethnologie, XLII, Berlin, 1910 (English trans. in Ann. Rep. Smithsonian Institution, Washington, 1911); Coomaraswamy, A.K., *Mediaeval Siṅhalese Art*, New York, 1956; Neogi, P., *Iron in Ancient India*, Calcutta, 1914. Steel may have been exported from India westwards well before the beginning of the Christian era. Quintus Curtius mentions that the chiefs of the Panjab presented Alexander with 100 talents of steel (*ferrum candidum*). The making of steel in small ingots by a true "Bessemer" process has survived in Southern India and Ceylon into the present century. If the early Vedic *ayas* refers to iron we might suppose that the use of iron weapons enabled the invaders to overcome the indigenous copper-using Dasyus.

16 Hornell, *loc. cit.* (the introduction of the coconut, of Pacific origin, and of the double-outrigger boat, due probably to the seafaring Malays who

case of the Kassites, who ruled in Babylonia about 1746-1180 B.C., and those of Aryan deities were in use amongst the Mitani people at Boghaz-Koi in Cappadocia about 1400 B.C.[17] The Aryans appear to have entered India between 2000 and 1500 B.C. through Afghanistan and the Hindu Kush, settling at first in the upper Indus valley, later in the upper Ganges valley, later still reaching the sea, the Vindhyas and the Narbadā, and still later penetrating to the Deccan and the far south.[18]

The Vedic Aryans were proficient in carpentry, building houses and racing chariots of wood; and in metal work, making vessels of *ayas*, presumably copper, for domestic and ritual use, and using gold jewellery. They wove, knew sewing and tanning, and made pottery. The early books afford no certain evidence for the making of images of any kind; on the other hand it is impossible to suppose that the manufactures alluded to above were devoid of significant decoration. In all probability, the early Aryan art was "decorative", or more accurately, abstract and symbolical; in other words, a Northern art in Strzygowski's sense.[19]

The probable character of early Aryan art at the time of the Indo-Iranian separation has been brilliantly visualized by the same writer; he applies to this ancient art of Altai-Iran, whose cognates we should naturally expect to find in India, the name Mazdean. The dominating conception is that of Hvarena (the

colonised Madagascar, are referable to the later period of maritime expansion, about the beginning of the Christian era); Lévi, S., *Préaryen et prédravidien dans l'Inde*, J.A., CCIII, I, 1923, pp. 55-57.

17 The Hittite language has Indo-European affinities. A treatise by a Mitanian author on horse-breeding found at Boghaz-koi contains numerous Sanskrit words; the first breeders and trainers of horses seem to have been a Sanskrit-speaking race.

18 For recent general discussions of the Aryan question in India see *C.H.I.*, Chs. III and IV; and Jarl Charpentier in B.S.O.S., IV, 1, 1926; for excellent account see V. Gordon Child, *The Aryans*, London, 1926.

19 Strzygowski, J., *Orient oder Rome*, Leipzig, 1901; *Altai-Iran und Völkerwanderung*, Leipzig, 1917; *Origins of Christian Church Art*, Oxford, 1923; *Perso-Indian Landscape in Northern Art*, in "The influences of Indian Art," India Soc., London, 1925.

Indian Varuṇa), the power of Ahura-Mazda "that makes the running waters gush from springs, plants sprout from the soil, winds blow the clouds, and men come to birth" and "govern the courses of the sun, moon, and stars." The characteristic expression of such ideas is to be sought in a kind of landscape "originating in a philosophy of the universe, and based upon significance and form...not upon natural objects exactly reproduced." This Mazdean art should include landscapes showing the sun and clouds, the earth with its plants and herds, and the waters; river landscapes with formal trees; hunting scenes; and symbolic geometrical arrangements of birds, animals and plants. The use of ornamented textiles and decorative hangings, characteristic for nomad races, is also indicated; and these are the forerunners of mural decoration consisting of formal floral ornament enclosed in framed spaces, where the essential element is pattern rather than representation.[20] Landscape of this type, indeed, can be recognized on punch-marked coins, in early Buddhist reliefs, Ajaṇṭā, and Rajput paintings, and in types of folk-art used in ritual decoration[21] and in many textiles. Indian art and culture, in any case, are a joint creation of the Dravidian and Aryan genius, a welding together of symbolic and representative, abstract and explicit language and thought. Already at Bhārhut and Sāñcī the Aryan symbol is yielding to its environment and passing into decoration; Kuṣāṇa art, with the fact of imagery and its roots in *bhakti,* is essentially Dravidian. Already, however, the Indra-Śānti figure at Bodh Gayā shows Aryan affecting Dravidian modes of expression, anticipating the essential qualities of all later *sāttvik* images. The Gupta Buddhas, Elephanta Maheśvara, Pallava *liṅgams,* and later Naṭarājas, are all products of the crossing of two spiritual natures; there is an originally realistic intention, but accommodated to the terms of pure design.

20 Strzygowski, *Perso-Indian Landscape in Northern Art,* in "The influences of Indian Art," India Soc., London, 1925.

21 Tagore, A.N., *L'Alpona, ou les Decorations rituelles au Bengale,* Paris, 1921; Annandale, N., *Plant and Animal Designs in the Mural Decoration of an Uriya Village,* M.A.S.B., VIII, 4, 1924.

Every icon is thus at once a symbol and a representation; the worshipper, though he knows that the deity takes the forms that are imagined by his worshippers, is nevertheless persuaded that the form is like the deity. Just in the same way the ascetic and sensual, opposed in primitive thought, and all other pairs of opposites, are theoretically and emotionally reconciled in mediaeval philosophy and faith. This in a very real sense was a "marriage of the East and West," or North and South, consummated, as the donors of an image would say "for the good of all sentient beings": a result, not of a superficial blending of Hellenistic and Indian technique, but of the crossing of spiritual tendencies, racial *saṁskāras* (preoccupations), that may well have been determined before the use of metals was known.

CHAPTER THREE

THE ŚAIŚUNĀGA-NANDA PERIOD

(642 - 320 B.C.)

A DEFINITELY historical period may be said to begin with the first half of the sixth century B.C. The kings of two dynasties ruling in Magadha include the Śaiśunāgas (*ca.* 642-413 B.C.) and the Nandas (*ca.* 413-322 B.C.); of the former, Bimbisāra (Śreṇika), the builder of New Rājagṛha, and Ajātaśatru (Kuṇika), the founder of Pāṭaliputra, were contemporaries of Mahāvīra and Buddha. The period is that of the later Vedic literature (*Brāhmaṇas, Upaniṣads,* and earlier *Sūtras*), and for the latter part of it the Buddhist *Jātakas* afford evidence. Vedic literature shows little or no knowledge of the West; but Darius in the sixth century B.C. had annexed a part of the Indus valley, and in the time of Alexander's invasion (327 B.C.) the Indus was still the boundary between India and Persia. Vast areas of the Panjab and in Sind, now arid, were then still rich and prosperous.

The later Vedic books show that a knowledge of the metals had advanced; tin, lead, and silver are mentioned as well as two varieties of *ayas,* usually regarded as copper and iron. Cotton, linen, silk and woollen garments were worn; a linen robe used in the Rājasūya ceremony was embroidered with representations of ritual vessels. Storeyed buildings are mentioned (*Ṛgveda Saṁhitā,* 6,46,9).[22] Round and square huts, bricks, plates, cups and spoons of gold and silver, iron knives, needles, mirrors, elevated bedsteads, thrones and seats, musical instruments, millstones, cushions, turbans (worn by the king in the Rājasūya ceremony, by students after graduation and by Vrātyas), crowns, jewellery, earthenware and a ship are mentioned in connection with the rituals. Writings, no doubt an early form

22 For Vedic references to architecture, see Ganguly, M., *Indian Architecture from the Vedic Period,* J.B.O.R.S., XII, 1926.

of the Brāhmī character, must have been known in the eighth century B.C. or earlier, but mnemonic methods were preferred for handing down the sacred texts.

The *Jātakas*, etc. describe the organization of craftsmen in gilds, eighteen in number, including "the woodworkers, the smiths, the leather-dressers, the painters and the rest, expert in various crafts." The smiths, workers in any metal, were already called *kammāra*, a name by which the higher craftsmen are still known in the south and in Ceylon. As in Ceylon, too, a characteristic localisation of industries in craft-villages is indicated; in towns, a further localisation in streets and quarters. Ivory workers amongst others are mentioned.[23]

Actual remains of pre-Maurya date, apart from the prehistoric antiquities above referred to, are comparatively few. The cyclopean walls of Old Rājagṛha are undoubtedly very ancient. Excavation of what are apparently Vedic burial-mounds of the seventh or eighth century B.C. at Lauṛiyā-Nandangaṛh have yielded amongst other objects a small repoussé gold plaque (Fig. 7) bearing the figure of a nude female. M. Jouveau-Dubreuil believes that he has discovered in Kerala (Malabar) rock-cut tombs of Vedic age. The most remarkable type is the "hollow stūpa with central column", a circular chamber, hemispherical in section, and with a very slender central pillar, apparently representing the centre pole of a tent or thatched hut, extending from floor to roof. A similar tomb is described by Longhurst; other caves by Logan, including another circular type with an opening or buffer in the roof.[24]

Minor antiquities of undoubted pre-Mauryan date have been found at various sites, of which the Bhiṛ mound at Taxila is the most important. The remains excavated here include beads and

23 Rhys Davids in *C.H.I.*, Ch. VIII, p. 206.

24 Jouveau-Dubreuil, *Vedic Antiquities*, Pondicherry, and London, 1922; Longhurst, A.H., *Rock-cut Tomb near Calicut*, A.S.I.-A.R., 1911-12; Logan, W., *Find of Ancient Pottery in Malabar*, Indian Antiquary, VIII; *Malabar*, Madras, 1887; the Vedic age of these interesting antiquities is doubtful: see Finot in B.E.F.E.O., 1922, p. 247, and Shastri in A.S.I.-A.R., 1922-23, p. 133.

lathe-turned polished hard stones, terracotta reliefs (some resembling the Earth goddess from Lauṛiyā referred to above) and two polished sandstone discs. The antiquities found here and elsewhere prove that glass-making had attained a high level before the Maurya period, and that the cutting and polishing of hard stones in the fourth and fifth centuries B.C. had reached a level of technical accomplishment which was sustained in the Maurya period, but never afterwards surpassed. Other terracottas of probably pre-Maurya date have been found at Nagarī, Bhīṭā, Basāṛh, and Pāṭaliputra.[25]

EARLY ASIATIC

The Indo-Sumerian and Indo-Iranian background outlined in the preceding chapters naturally prepares us for the recognition of many common elements in Early Indian and Western Asiatic art. And in fact a great variety of motifs found in Maurya, Śuṅga and early Āndhra art, and thus antedating the age of Hellenistic influence, present a Western Asiatic appearance, suggesting parallels in Sumerian, Hittite, Assyrian, Mykenean, Cretan, Trojan, Lykian, Phoenician, Achaemenid and Scythian cultures. A partial list of such motifs would include such mythical monsters as winged lions, centaurs, griffons, tritons; animals formally posed in profile with head forward, facing, or turned back, animals addorsed and affronted, animal combats and friezes; the sun car with four horses; the bay wreath and mural crown; altar or battlement friezes of Bhārhut and Orissa; the tree of life; mountain and water formulae; palmette and honeysuckle (blue lotus), rosette and petal-moulding (rose lotus), acanthus, reel and bead; lotus or "bell" (so-called "Persepolitan") capital, volute capital; Troy mark and other symbols on punch-marked coins. These and others, such as the fret, spiral, volute, labyrinth and *svastika* have survived in folk art up to modern times and are widely distributed in India and Ceylon.[26]

25 For the antiquities of the Bhiṛ mound see A.S.I.-A.R., 1919-20 and 1920-21.

26 The material is too abundant to be cited in detail; see amongst other sources Birdwood, Sir George, *Industrial Arts of India,* London, 1880,

A striking example is afforded by the group of designs representing two or more animals having but one head, so placed as to be equally appropriate to each of the several bodies. Designs of lions of this type occur on an Etruscan vase of the sixth century B.C., on a Śuṅga railing pillar from Gaṛhwā, and in eighteenth century Siṅhalese folk art.[27] A design of four deer is even more remarkable; it occurs on a Chalcidian vase of the sixth century B.C. (derived, no doubt, as Morin-Jean suggests, from an oriental textile), then on a capital of Cave I at Ajaṇṭā (Fig. 8), in a Rajput drawing of the nineteenth century, and finally in Southern India in the eighteenth and twentieth centuries.[28] A reverse type is illustrated by the two-headed bird which first appears in Hittite art at Boghaz-Koi, then on a Jaina *stūpa* base at Taxila, later as a common Saracenic and European armorial device, as well as in Southern India and in Siṅhalese folk art.[29]

pp. 325 ff.; Coomaraswamy, *Some Ancient Elements in Indian Decorative Art,* O.Z., II, 1913; Cunningham, A., *The Stupa of Bharhut,* London, 1879, *Mahābodhi, or the Great Buddhist Temple at Buddhagaya,* London, 1892. The Hittites, *ca.* 1700-1200 B.C. played a considerable part in developing Babylonian designs and transmitting them to the Eastern Mediterranean; most likely it is more for this reason than because of direct connections that Indo-Hittite and Indo-Lydian parallels can be recognized, the forms being cognate in West and East. The *svastika* appears in the lowest strata at Susa, and occurs commonly on seals from Mohenjo-Daro, the double-headed eagle is early Chaldean. For the early motifs see Pottier, *Délégation en Perse,* vol. 13. Animals with interlacing necks are Sumerian (Weber, O., *Ein siberner Zeptergriff aus Syrien,* Jahrb. d. preuss. Kunsts., 1915, p. 59, fig. 14). Indian numerals are used in ancient Hittite texts (Jensen, P., in Sitz. k. bairische Ak., Wiss., Berlin., 1919, pp. 367 ff.).

27 Morin-Jean, *Dessin des animaux en Grèce d'après les vases peints,* Paris, 1911; Cunningham, *Archaeological Survey Reports,* vol. X, pl. V; Coomaraswamy, *Some Ancient Elements in Indian Decorative Art,* O.Z., II, 1913; cf. Martin, F.R., *Miniature Painters of Persia, India and Turkey,* 1912, pl. 164; Sarre and Mittwoch, *Zeichnungen von Riza Abbasi,* München, 1914, pl. 11; British Museum Ms. Or. 2529. f. 141; Museum of Fine Arts, Boston, Rajput drawing no. 25, 531.

28 Morin-Jean, *loc. cit.,* 154; Coomaraswamy, *Rajput Drawing,* M. F.A., Boston, no. 26, 50.

29 Springer, Anton, *Kunstgeschichte,* Leipzig, 1923, fig. 177; Marshall,

The cylindrical *stūpa* with drum in two stages, as seen at Beḍsā and in the Kuṣāṇa period is identical in form with a Phoenician tomb at Amrith (Marath) in North Syria.[30] The Bhārhut altar or battlement-frieze occurs as a string course on the same tomb and on a Babylonian *kudurru*.[31] Lydian excavated and monolithic tombs at Pinara and Xanthos on the south coast of Asia Minor present some analogy with the early Indian rock-cut *caitya*-halls; but the Lydian door jambs are erect.[32] The true arch, which is widely if sparsely distributed in India long before the Muhammadan period, occurs in Sumerian and other Mesopotamian sites.[33]

Another parallel is afforded by the occurrence of shoulder wings (Figs. 9, 20) on certain terracottas and figures of deities found in India.[34] An early Indian terracotta type of female divinity closely resembles a form found at Ur.[35]

Other analogies are technical: thus, the art of granulating gold, which may have originated in Egypt in the sixth dynasty, and is highly characteristic of Trojan, Mykenean and later pre-

J., *Guide to Taxila*, p. 74, Calcutta, 1918; Coomaraswamy, *Mediaeval Siṅhalese art*, 1956, N.Y.

30 Springer, *loc. cit.*, fig. 193; Perrot et Chipiez, *Phénicechypre* (*Hist. de l'art dans l'antiquate*, Paris, 1882-1914), fig. 95; against this analogy is the fact that the *early* stūpas are always hemispherical.

31 Springer, *loc. cit.*, Delaporte, L., *La Mésopotamie*, Paris, 1923, fig. 11. The form occurs in India not only in the frieze, but as an altar and as a battlement. Cf. *Mohenjo-Daro*, pl. CLV, 33.

32 Springer, *loc. cit.*, figs. 188, 191.

33 Sumerian examples, see Perrot et Chipiez, *loc. cit.*, fig. 55; Wooley, C.L., *Excavations at Ur*, Antiquities Journal, V, London, 1925, p. 387, and pls. XXXVII and XLV.

34 Spooner, D.B., *Excavations at Basāṛh*, A.S.I.-A.R., 1913-1914, p. 116 and pl. XLIV (Basāṛh); Vogel, J. Ph., *The Mathurā School of Sculpture*, A.S.I.-A.R., 1906-07 and 1909-10, pl. XXVIII, c and 13, p. 104 (Sūrya, D 46 in the Mathurā Museum); A.S.I.-A.R., 1922-23, pl. X, b (bronze goddess from Akum Ḍherī). Sir John Evans in Journ. Hellenic Studies, XLIV, 1925, pt. 1, states that the sacral knots on the shoulders of the Minoan goddess became the shoulder wings of Greek art.

35 C.B.S. 15634 in the Philadelphia University Museum, from the cemetery of Diqdiqqeh near Ur, assigned to 2400-200 B.C.

Christian Mediterranean cultures, is typical of the gold jewellery found at many early Buddhist sites in India, e.g., Toṛdher in the Yusufzai district and Piprāhwa in Nepal, and equally of modern Tamil and Siṅhalese jewellery in Ceylon.[36] On the other hand the art of encrusting gems seems to be of Indian origin, not appearing in the Mediterranean until after the time of Alexander.[37] The beaten pottery technique of the eastern Mediterranean has been recognized at Chārsada, and is represented by ancient and modern practice in Ceylon.[38] Early Indian and Assyrian glass are of similar composition.[39]

Thus, so far as its constituent elements are concerned, and apart from any question of style, there is comparatively little in Indian decorative art that is peculiar to India, and much that India shares with Western Asia.

In view of the fact that the forms referred to appear in Indian art for the first time in the Maurya and Śuṅga periods and that there is good evidence of Achaemenid influence at this time, it has been not unusual to assume that the whole group of Western Asiatic and Persian motifs came into India in the Maurya period.[40] It must, however, be constantly borne in mind that a motif was not necessarily invented or borrowed at the date of its first appearance in permanent material; indeed, a first appearance in stone is almost tantamount to proof of an earlier currency in wood. No one, in fact, doubts the existence of a pre-Maurya Indian art of sculpture and architecture in wood, clay modelling, ivory carving, cutting of hard stone, glass, textiles and metal work, and this art must have embraced an extensive ensemble of decorative motifs, ranging from lines and dots incised or painted on earthen pots and chank bangles to representations

36 Marshall, *Buddhist Gold Jewellery*, A.S.I.-A.R., 1902-03; Coomaraswamy, *Mediaeval Siṅhalese Art*, 1956, pls. XLIII-L.

37 Marshall, A.S.I.-A.R., 1902-03; Coomaraswamy, in Spolia Zeylanica, (technique) vol. VI and I, pls. XLVIII, L.

38 Marshall and Vogel, *Excavations at Chārdasa*, A.S.I.-A.R., 1902-03, p. 181; Coomaraswamy, *Mediaeval Siṅhalese Art*, p. 220.

39 A.S.I.-A.R., 1923-24, p. 115.

40 According to Jouveau-Dubreuil, *Archeologie de Sud de l'Inde*, vol. 1, p. 25, in the time of Darius.

of the human figure. To suppose that the whole group of motifs of Western Asiatic aspect was introduced by Aśoka's Persian craftsmen *en bloc* would thus necessarily imply a belief in the existence of a lost pre-Maurya art of some strange and unknown kind. As a matter of fact, it would be fantastic to postulate the existence of any such art, and, in view of our knowledge of the continuous preservation of motifs, and the conservative character of Indian decorative art, it would be impossible to believe that it could have vanished without trace.

All this amounts to proof that the themes and motifs of pre-Maurya art cannot have differed very greatly from those of Maurya and Śuṅga; fantastic animals, palmettes, rosettes, and bell capitals must have been common elements of the craftsman's repertory under the Nandas as in the time of Aśoka. India, in centuries and perhaps millenniums B.C., was an integral part of an "Ancient East" that extended from the Mediterranean to the Ganges valley. In this ancient world there prevailed a common type of culture, which may well have had a continuous history extending upwards from the stone age. Some of its most widely distributed decorative, or more accurately speaking, symbolic motifs, such as the spiral and *svastika*, with certain phases of its mythology, such as the cults of Sun and Fire, Yakṣas and Nāgas, and of a nude goddess may go back to that remote past; more sophisticated motifs and technical discoveries may have originated in any part of the area; a majority, perhaps in southern Mesopotamia,[41] others in India or in Egypt.

The effect of these considerations is to withdraw India from its isolation; as a background to the existing art there is a "common early Asiatic art, which has left its uttermost ripple marks alike on the shores of Hellas, the extreme west of Ireland,

41 Pottier, E., *Les Sumeriens et la Chaldée,* Rev. de l'art ancient et moderne, XXVII, 1910: "La Chaldée nous apparait comme le reservoir d'ou les formules d'art le plus connues se sont deversées sur le mond entier"; and Rostovtzeff, M., *Iranians and Greeks in South Russia,* Oxford, 1922, pp. 192, 193, 237: "All these types spread far and wide, eastward, westward and northward."

Etruria, Phoenicia, Egypt, India, and China."[42] All that belongs to this phase of art is equally the common inheritance of Europe and Asia, and its various forms as they occur in India or elsewhere at various periods up to the present day are to be regarded as cognates rather than as borrowings.

42 Okakura, K., *Ideals of the East*, 2nd ed., London, 1904. Cf. Marshall in A.S.I.-A.R., 1923-24, p. 49, and de Morgan, J., *L'Egypte et l'Asie aux temps antehistoriques*, J.A. CCIII, 1923.

CHAPTER FOUR

VEDIC ORIGINS

EARLY vedic religion—the religion of the Aryans in Northern India—consisted in the worship of the personified powers of Nature, in particular of Agni, Indra, Sūrya, Varuṇa, Viṣṇu, Rudra and Yama. These and other powers and beings were anthropomorphically conceived and are described as wearing garments, carrying weapons and driving in cars; they were worshipped with hymns and sacrifices, that they might bless and protect their worshippers. Magical incantations were employed to the same ends. The spirits of the ancestors were likewise invoked and served with offerings. The ritual grew in complication and came to lie almost entirely in the hands of expert priests (Brāhmaṇas), amongst whom the sacred texts were handed down orally in pupillary succession. There is no evidence, and little probability, that images of any of the deities were made, whether sculptured or painted.[43]

There existed also aboriginal (Dravidian) cults of various popular divinities, such as the Yakṣas, Nāgas and other nature-spirits not yet received into the Brāhmaṇical pantheon; of a primitive deity, afterwards identified with Śiva, whose followers are referred to in the *Ṛgveda* as worshippers of the Phallus-god (Śiśna-deva); and of the Earth and other female deities. The industrial arts were mainly in the hands of the non-Aryan communities. It is possible that rude images were employed in the popular cults. Wood and brick were used for building. Iron, copper, silver, gold and lead were known. Many of the decorative motifs with Iranian affinities which survive in folk art to the present day must already have been in use. The caste system existed only in embryo.

43 The golden *puruṣa* which formed a part of the altar of sacrifice and the effigy *kṛtya* of the magic rites were probably symbols, and not in any sense representations.

CHAPTER FIVE

PRE-MAURYAN SCULPTURE

THE early development of Indian sculpture and painting, like that of the drama, appears to have been connected with ancestor cults and hero-worship. The *Citra-lakṣaṇa*, an early Śilpaśāstra, now known only in the Tibetan translation in the Tanjur, is chiefly devoted to a prescription of the proper manner in which a Cakravartin should be represented: the canon is set 'for kings and other beings' (the gods). So far as the *lakṣaṇas* of the Cakravartin are concerned, the Śāstra probably dates back to pre-Buddhist times. In any case, the apotheosis of kings and the erection of funerary statues seem to have been characteristic of Indian civilization from the age of the earliest surviving monuments onwards. The oldest Indian sculpture so far known appears to be the well-known 'Parkham Statue' of the Mathurā Museum (Fig. 10), which bears, according to recent readings, an inscription referring to Kuṇika Ajātaśatru, of the Śaiśunāga dynasty, who died in 618 B.C. Closely related to this image is the female figure, perhaps a Yakṣī, from Besnagar, now in the Calcutta Museum. Two statues found at Patna bear the names of other Śaiśunāga emperors, Udayin and Nanda Vardhana, both of the fifth century B.C. The female caurī-bearer lately found at Dīdarganj, and now in the Patna Museum, may be equally early.

The group of figures above referred to, while implying a long anterior development in wood or other impermanent material, represents the genuinely primitive aspect of Indian art. The sense of this early art is not imaginative, but powerfully material. These human figures, over life-size, resting their immense weight firmly on the earth, are immediate and affirmative expressions of physical energy. Life is accepted without question or analysis: the solid flesh is not idealized. Neither philosophic introspection nor passionate devotion have yet affected art: there is no trace of romanticism or refinement. At the same time, this pre-Mauryan Indian art is not, like early Egyptian art, complete within itself, bounded by its material and representative achievement and of altogether mortal essence: it is not yet spiritual, rather than unspiritual.

Mr. Jayaswal's researches in the field of pre-Mauryan art have pointed the way to the most fruitful and the least explored sources for the origins of Indian art: this early sculpture in an absolutely pure mode, springing directly from the earth it stands upon, alone supplies the key to subsequent developments. Here, for example, lies the explanation of the almost complete submergence of Hellenistic formulae in the unified national schools of the Gupta age: we can follow from the seventh century B.C. to the sixth or seventh century A.D., and thence on, a continuous tradition; and we realise that this clear current flowed too powerfully and too immediately from native sources to have been seriously deflected by the foreign formulae which it adopted and moulded to its own ends.

The immediate evidence offered for the new interpretations of what were formerly regarded as works of Mauryan date is palaeographical, and still to some extent a matter of controversy; but the conclusions are amply supported by the internal aesthetic evidence, which clearly demands an earlier dating of the primitive sculptures. It would be indeed surprising if the most powerful and original elements of this art, destined to remain pre-potent for a millennium and a half, had not already found expression in the age of the great spiritual crisis. No lesser material force than this, no less complete and pure an acceptance of physical existence could have been a sure foundation for the Great Enlightenment—a term used here to designate, not merely the Mahāsambodhi of the Buddha, but the awakening of the race from innocence to consciousness implied in the passage from Vedic to Vedantic thought.

CHAPTER SIX

THE GREAT ENLIGHTENMENT

BY the eighth century B.C. philosophical speculation had advanced; the doctrines of *karma* and *saṁsāra* had come to be generally accepted; and, by contrast with the merely temporary advantage of rebirth in a heaven, salvation (*mokṣa, nirvāṇa*) from the conditions of mortality was recognized as the highest good. This salvation or spiritual freedom could only be attained with the immediate experience of spiritual truth, not through the Vedic ritual nor by works. The meaning of life was only to be found in the knowledge of the Self, in the identification of all that is known with the knowing subject. This was a revelation that determined the whole subsequent development of Indian civilization, alike in content and form. As such, it finds its first and purest expression in the Upaniṣads and, later, in Buddhism and Jainism and other individual systems. Historically, it is of Kṣatriya rather than of Brāhmaṇa origin. Its expression in the Upaniṣads, afterwards formulated as the Vedānta, however, was early accepted by the Brāhmaṇas as the consummation and goal of the Vedic tradition, and constitutes the spiritual background for the whole subsequent development of the monotheistic faiths and of the Hindu social order. Buddhism and Jainism, developing on parallel lines, although in formal opposition to Hindu systems, long survived as heterodox persuasions —the former in Southern India until the seventh century, and in Bengal until the end of the twelfth, the latter to the present day.

It will be convenient here to summarise the formulation of truth according to the leading systems of the Enlightenment:

UPANIṢADS : Identity of the individual consciousness (not the empirical ego) with the unknowable Supreme Self or Brahman which is 'not so,' the innermost principle of the Universe; unreality of the latter as extended in time and space, and consequently merely relative truth of doctrines of creation, transmigration, etc.

BUDDHISM : Association of existence with suffering; impermanence and causal origination of all phenomena, non-existence of any ego.

SĀṄKHYA : Illusory association of plurality of knowing subjects (Puruṣa) with Nature, actual and potential (Prakṛti); the three factors, *sattva, rajas* and *tāmasa*, of the objective world.

JAINISM : Soul (*jīva*) and non-soul (*ajīva*) linked by *karma*.

Sannyāsa (asceticism), *Tapas* (penance) and *Yoga* (concentration of thought) are favoured by all these systems, in so far as they accommodate themselves to the concept of causality, as practical 'means' tending to realization.

None of these systems, in their origin, implied a cult of personal divinities, still less did they require a use of images. Even the *Yoga* mentions the Lord (Īśvara) only as one among other suitable objects of meditation. For another reason, it was impossible that immediate effects of the Enlightenment should have been recognized in art: the mode of life at first associated with the conception of spiritual freedom is ascetic; and the explicit and implicit tendency of all the philosophic systems at this time is to regard the arts (which had never yet been thought of as media for the expression of spiritual ideas) exclusively in their sensual aspect as means of enjoyment—and as the *Mārkaṇḍeya Purāṇa* later expresses it, 'Nothing should be done by a Brāhmaṇa for the sake of enjoyment.' Cāṇakya classes musicians and actors with courtesans; Manu forbids the householder to dance or sing, and reckons architects and actors amongst unworthy men who should not be invited to sacrifices. In early Buddhist literature the painter is compared to the purveyor of aphrodisiacs; the Buddha even condemns the presentation of the Dhamma in an attractive literary form. And, in fact, the actual themes of artistic representation in this age cannot have been such as to invite the approval of those whose faces were turned away from the world. Only at a much later period was there a conscious expression of spiritual ideas through plastic art, and only later still a distinction drawn between the sympathetic value and the spiritual content even of literary works.

CHAPTER SEVEN

EARLY BUDDHIST ART—MAURYA, ŚUṄGA AND EARLY ĀNDHRA

ART of the Mauryan period may be said to exhibit three main phases : (1) the continuation of the pre-Mauryan tradition, now applied in some instances to the representation of Vedic deities; the most striking illustration of this development is afforded by the sculptured reliefs of Sūrya and Indra (Fig. 14) in the veranda of the ancient *vihāra* at Bhājā; (2) the court art of Aśoka, typically seen in the monolithic columns (Fig. 12) on which are inscribed his famous edicts, and in which foreign (Iranian) elements predominate; and (3) the beginnings of brick and stone architecture, as in the case of the original *stūpa* at Sāñcī, the small monolithic rail at Sāñcī, and the Lomas Ṛṣi 'cave' in the Barābar hills near Bodh Gayā, with its ornamented façade, reproducing the forms of wooden structure.

The beginnings of Buddhist art appear to be associated with the memorial monuments (*caityas*) erected on the sites of the Four Great Events of the Buddha's life and in other places. Funeral mounds (*stūpas*) were, indeed, already erected over the divided remains immediately after the cremation of the Buddha's body and he himself, before his death, is recorded to have spoken of 'four places which an Aryan worshipper should visit with religious emotion'. Each of the Great Events and sites was represented by a symbol, and these symbols, taken collectively, relate, in a kind of pictorial shorthand, the whole story of the Buddha's life. Most of them occur abundantly on the punch-marked coins of the fourth and fifth centuries B.C.; a few appear for the first time at Bhārhut and Sāñcī, and the majority survive in Indian Buddhist art to the end, side by side with the later developments. In the following table are given the sites, significant events and symbols :

PLACE	EVENT	SYMBOL
Kapilavastu	Conception	Elephant
	Nativity	Lotus, bull
	Going Forth	Gate, horse
Bodh Gayā	Great Enlightenment	Bodhi tree with rail
Sārnāth	First Preaching	Wheel, often with deer
Kuśinagara	Final *Nirvāṇa* (Death)	*Stūpa*

To the Śuṅga period (185-80 B.C.) must be assigned (approximately in chronological order) the sculptured railings and gateway at Bhārhut, the stone casing, ground balustrade and plain railing at Sāñcī, the sculptured railings at Bodh Gayā, certain fragments at Mathurā, the earliest sculptures at Amarāvatī, and also the *caitya*-hall or churches at Guntupalle, Bhājā, Koṇḍāne, Pitālkhorā, Ajaṇṭā (Cave X), Beḍsā, Ajaṇṭā (Cave IX), and the early Jaina caves at Udayagiri in Orissa. Taken collectively, the total amount of relief sculpture at these sites is very considerable. Sculpture in the round is hardly represented.

Except at Bhārhut, however, the greater part of the sculpture seems to be secular or decorative, rather than definitely religious, particularly so in the case of the Jaina caves in Orissa (where however, there occur representations of Sūrya and of Māyā Devī or Gajalakṣmī); but this may be due to our inability to recognize the subject-matter. At Bhārhut the most important Buddhist sculptures are the numerous medallions illustrating Jātaka stories, each with an identifying inscription; reliefs illustrating historical episodes of the Buddha's life; and pillars bearing in relief the figures of guardian *yakṣas* and *yakṣīs, nāga* kings and *devatās*—the nature spirits of popular cults embraced by Buddhist mythology and regarded as defenders of the faith. The Jātaka reliefs are excellent pieces of condensed storytelling, the representation of trees and landscape full of interest and decorative beauty, the animals and human figures well understood and placed, whether singly or in groups. The Śuṅga sculptures at Sāñcī, on the other hand, are mainly decorative. That of the early caves, though always in relief, is exceedingly massive in character and very clearly related to pre-Mauryan art.

It has been remarked of Mauryan and Śuṅga art by Sir John Marshall that the sculptor was still bound by the law of frontality (i.e., considering the composition from only one point of view) and that "the 'memory picture' had not yet given place to direct observation of nature". The first remark is obviously true as a fact of technical procedure; the second involves a certain misinterpretation of Indian aesthetic psychology and deserves a longer discussion. The memory picture—or rather, a synthetic image based on past experience—is from first to last the essential foundation of Indian art: we cannot recognize here any such innate striving towards realism as that which becomes apparent, soon after the primitive developments, in Greek and Christian art. The Indian method is always one of visualization—unconscious in primitive, systematized in the mature art. Indian art is always a language employing symbols, valid only by tradition and convention. The symbol may be little more than a geometrical design, as in the case of the lotus rosette denoting miraculous birth, or anthropomorphic as in the later Nativities, where Māyā Devī is represented as a woman, either with or without the infant Bodhisattva. In both cases equally, there is definite and comprehensible statement; but the form of the statement is always that of the art language of the day (we may illustrate this by pointing out that perspective representation is a part of the art language of our own times, while it does not by itself make modern art superior to ancient art); and this language is never one of 'direct observation of nature'. It is true that a tendency to realism is evident in the Gandhāra sculptures, but there it is of Western origin, and it does not prevail in Indian or Chinese art which preserve the formulae alone, and not the intention of Greco-Buddhist sculpture. On the other hand, we do recognize in Indian art of certain periods and miss at other times a certain virtuous and moving, indeed an essential, quality which is often spoken of as true to Nature: the development of this truth we describe as progress, the loss of it as decadence, but it must not be confused with the assimilation of the symbol to natural appearance, which, by itself, is a technical and not an aesthetic progress. The point to be made is that this truth is not the result of observation (of models) but of feeling (empathy, *einfühlung, sādhārṇa,* with reference to the artist in the first instance, rather than the critic). If we are impressed by the truth of a movement in sculpture or painting, this means, not that the craftsman has *observed* the movement (however familiar he may be with it in daily life), but that at the time of the conception and execution of his work, he has *felt* the corresponding tensions in his own flesh. The 'awkwardness', then, of primitive art, is that of undeveloped consciousness (self-awareness), progress, the evidence of increasing consciousness, and decadence of apathy. It is in this way that a nation's art reveals the various stages of its spiritual history. Technical perfection, on the other hand, is a matter of knowledge and skill, rather than of vitality : aesthetically neither good nor bad, it need not and often does not coincide with the perfection of art.

The splendid gateways of the Sāñcī *stūpa* were erected under the patronage of Āndhra kings, probably between 70 and 50 B.C. Their surfaces are covered with reliefs illustrating historical scenes from the Buddha's life, a few Jātaka stories, and with representations of guardian *yakṣas* and *yakṣīs* (some in relief, some in the round), animals, Buddhist symbols and decorative designs. An exquisite terracotta plaque from Bhīṭā, probably from an ivory die, is identical in style with the reliefs of the Sāñcī gateways. The Sāñcī reliefs present a very detailed and animated picture of Indian life, invaluable to the student of culture, even apart from their value as art. The sculptors—technically carvers in wood and ivory, though working now in stone—are far more skilful and experienced than heretofore; that is to say, their knowledge and facility are greater, the cutting of the reliefs is deeper, the composition more sophisticated, the sense of perspective and depth much more convincing. But the spiritual quality of the art remains unchanged. Even when the theme is altogether Buddhist, the art remains innocent, untroubled, and even sensuous, and neither intellectual nor idealistic. Mediaeval Buddhist art is often the work of Buddhist monks; but early Buddhist art is the art of the people, used for the glorification of religion, telling the story of Buddhism in the clearest and simplest possible way, and never attempting the embodiment of spiritual ideals in terms of form. When the theme is less precisely Buddhist—as in the representations of *yakṣas* and *yakṣīs* at Bhārhut and Sāñcī, and on the railing pillars of the Jaina *stūpa* at Mathurā (also of the first century B.C.)—the inherent sensuousness, and even sensuality, of the art becomes more obvious still: an interpretation of spiritual love as a manifestation or symbol, and of the whole physical world as a theophany, belongs to a much later phase of thought, and we cannot be surprised that Buddhist monks were warned to turn away their eyes from 'conversation' pictures, which must have been love scenes of the sort we find amongst the paintings of Ajaṇṭā and in later Hindu sculpture. Only in the devoted gesture of worshipping figures kneeling before the *bodhi*-trees or empty thrones is there any trace of spiritual passion.

No Buddha image appears in early Buddhist art; and even in the historical scenes, the Buddha's presence is indicated, not by a human representation, but by the formal symbols already mentioned, together with a few others, particularly the footprints (*pādukā*) or umbrella (*chattra*). In the Bhārhut 'Descent from the Tuṣita Heaven', for example, we see only the threefold ladder, with one footprint at the top, another at the bottom. In the elaborate scene of the 'Going Forth' at Sāñcī, Siddhārtha's presence is indicated, at five successive stages of the outward journey, only by the honorific parasol borne beside the riderless horse; remaining in the forest, his presence is indicated by footprints; attaining Enlightenment, by the railed Tree of Wisdom. The Nativity is illustrated by the lotus, bull or elephant, and in another way (also at Bhārhut) by the seated figure of Māyā Devī, with the two elephants pouring water from inverted jars—a picture of the bathing of the new-born child, in which the child is not seen. On the other hand, in Jātaka representations, the sculptors are perfectly well able, and do not hesitate, to represent the Bodhisattva in human shape where the story requires it. The explanation of the absence of the human Buddha figure from the historical scenes appears to lie, not in any inability to represent the Master in an appropriate manner, but in the existence of an already familiar method of indicating the Great Events of the Buddha's life by means of symbols. The sculptors of Bhārhut and Sāñcī had large spaces to cover : they fill their story by the method of continuous narration (the representation of successive scenes in which the same actors appear again and again), with abundant detail and perfect logic—but only, as it were, by filling in the spaces between the already well-known symbols. And as regards the separate image, it is evident that the apotheosis of the Buddha had not yet, at least in orthodox circles, proceeded so far as to necessitate the use of an icon.

SELECT BIBLIOGRAPHY

Cunningham, A. : *The Stupa of Bharhut*. London, 1879.

Foucher, A. : *The Beginnings of Buddhist Art*. London, 1918.

Konow, Sten : *Note on the Use of Images in Ancient India*, Indian Antiquary, Vol. XXXVIII, 1909.

Maisey, F.C. : *Sanchi and its Remains*. London, 1892.

Marshall, J.H. : *Guide to Sanchi*. Calcutta, 1918.

Rapson, E.J. (ed.) : *Cambridge History of India*, Vol. 1.

Taki, Seiichi : *An Example of the Earliest Indian Painting*. Kokka Magazine, Tokio, No. 355, 1919.

Waddell, L.A. : *Evolution of the Buddhist Cult, its Gods, Images and Art*. *Imperial and Asiatic Quarterly Review*, 1912.

Buddha's Diadem or 'Uṣṇīṣa'. Ostasiatische Zeitschrift, Vol. 3, Berlin, 1915.

CHAPTER EIGHT

DEVELOPMENT OF DEVOTIONAL THEISM

THE development which we have so far followed in Buddhism and Buddhist art is a special phase of the contemporary evolution of Indian thought and religion as a whole. The apparent predominance of Buddhist art is mainly due to special circumstances of patronage and consequent abundant production in certain centres and not to any real submergence of the Brāhmaṇical tradition. To take a concrete case, which really covers the whole ground ('since what is not to be found in the *Mahābhārata* is not to be found in India'), the development of the Epics must have been continuous from the days of their existence in ballad form (1000 to 500 B.C.) to that of their final recension about the fourth century A.D. The first expansion of the *Mahābhārata*, for example, in which Śiva and Viṣṇu, side by side with Brahmā, are already regarded as the supreme gods, Hindu temples as well as Buddhist *stūpas* are mentioned and the *Bhagavad-Gītā* appears, belongs to the three centuries between the Mauryan and Kuṣāṇa periods: the final stage, with its complete statement of Hindu *dharma* and social organization, belongs to the Kuṣāṇa and early Gupta periods. In the same way the law books, particularly of Manu, and the technical literature, such as Bharata's *Nāṭyaśāstra*, imply development long preceding the final recensions. And in just the same way the appearance of Hindu sculpture and architecture in the Kuṣāṇa and early Gupta period, even in the absence of all other evidence, would prove a lengthy previous development. The sum of Indian culture in the Gupta period, already essentially Hindu rather than Buddhist, is so rich, so fully organised, and so conscious, that we can hardly fail to regard the preceding half a millennium as the period of highest creative activity in the whole development of Hindu civilization—an activity to be regarded as the formal and material embodiment of the Great Enlightenment.

We observe, meanwhile, the gradual emergence of Śiva and Viṣṇu as the supreme powers, followed by the recognition of aboriginal and local deities, including the goddesses, as aspects of one Overlord (Īśvara), the ultimate object of all devotion. In the *Bhagavad-Gītā* we find, in the words of Kṛṣṇa : 'Abandoning all duties, come unto Me'; and of devotees who worship other gods, says Kṛṣṇa, 'they also worship Me'. The fundamental characteristic of the embodiment, determination or interpretation of the spiritual impulse is, in fact, to be recognized in the rise of the theistic cults, with their doctrine and practice of devotion (*bhakti*), and here lay the immediate necessity determining the development of a religious art.

This is not the place in which to trace in any detail the beginnings of the theistic cults. It need only be remarked that in the time of the Buddha the most honoured name is that of Brahmā, and in Buddhist literature the Brāhmaṇical pantheon is represented almost exclusively by Brahmā and Indra, while the latter appears no less frequently in Jaina literature and art. Brahmā and Indra are the only deities represented in the Greco-Buddhist art of Gandhāra, and the forms of certain of the Bodhisattvas appear to be derived from these Indian prototypes. Neither of these gods is the object of any widespread cult in later times: there we find only the great gods Śiva and Viṣṇu, and the goddess Devī, in their innumerable forms and manifestations. Sūrya is the only one of the old Vedic deities who remains an exalted power, with an extended cult and iconography.

The germs of almost all later forms of Hindu thought are to be traced in the Upaniṣads, which have been interpreted by each school in its own way; and, just as the process of formulation and definition of Hindu systems was going on side by side with the doctrinal development and sectarian subdivision of Buddhism, so is it clear that Hindu art was developing under similar conditions. Monuments were erected in honour of particular deities; an example of this is afforded by the inscribed pillar at Besnagar erected by Heliodorus in the second century B.C., where Vasudeva is described as the God of Gods. It is evident that the religion of the Bhāgavatas was by this time fully established; but that, just as in Buddhism, the deities were first represented by symbols (here the Garuḍadhvaja) rather than by images. We gather, however, from Patañjali, commentator on Pāṇini in the second century B.C., that images of Śiva, Skanda and Viśākha were already exhibited and sold. We have already spoken of the early Vedic reference to liṅga worshippers; and we may well suppose that phallic symbols, particularly the erect pillar, were made use of as cult objects at an early date. The liṅgam was now adopted into orthodox faith and has remained to this day the general *avyakta* symbol of Śiva. The stone liṅgam discovered by the late T.A. Gopinatha Rao at Guḍimallam, a five foot monolith consisting of the liṅgam proper and an anthropomorphic image, is not only the earliest known (first or second century B.C.) image of a Hindu deity and thus of the highest historical interest, but a sculpture of amazing force and extraordinary technical accomplishment (Fig. 16). The figure of the deity stands upright in high relief against the underside of the erect phallus, his feet supported by a crouching *yakṣa* or *rākṣasa*; he wears a thin muslin *dhoti* clearly revealing the form beneath, and heavy jewels, including ear-rings, necklace, bracelets and anklets. There is no sacred thread. The hair is inter-braided with strands of flowers, and wound about the head like a turban. The eyes slant rather upwards, and the cheek bones are high—a Dravidian rather than an Aryan type. The material is a reddish igneous rock, the surface highly polished. The deity is two-armed, holding in one hand a ram, in the other a water-pot and an axe (*paraśu*), whence the liṅgam is known as the Paraśurāmeśvara liṅgam. It will be seen at once that this is a work in the immediate tradition of older Indian art, pre-Mauryan and Bhārhut: the drapery recalls that of the figure of Kuṇika Ajātaśatru (Fig. 10), the yakṣa *vāhana* is almost identical with the yakṣa of the Bhārhut Kuvera pediment (Fig. 15). The head-dress and jewellery too are reminiscent of Bhārhut. But this is a more fully developed art there is greater muscular tension and consequently a more evident activity, while the facial expression latent in early sculpture is now intentional.

An early *mukhaliṅgam* from Bhīṭā, now in the Lucknow Museum, bears an inscription in characters assignable to the first century B.C. The top of the pillar is shaped as the head and shoulders of a male, holding a vase in his left hand, while the right is raised in *abhaya hasta*. Below this bust are represented on the shaft of the liṅgam four heads in low relief.

The sense of devotion to a personal god is a general tendency, by no means exclusively Hindu, but affecting equally the forms of Buddhist belief, and to a less extent the Jaina. A veritable transformation of Buddhism had been taking place in the Mauryan, Śuṅga and early Āndhra periods. Whereas in primitive Buddhism the Buddha was a man who had attained enlightenment and who after death was no longer subject to the conditions of existence, he came to be regarded in the Mahāyāna as the embodiment or incarnation of a principle. He comes, in fact, to be regarded as a god, and with what passionate devotion he is adored may be judged from the worshipping figures of the Amarāvatī reliefs. Not only is the Buddha thus deified, but a pantheon of Buddhist deities arises, over and above the already well-known Buddhist forms of the Hindu Brahmā and Indra, and the Yakṣas and Nāgas who are admitted to the cult of Buddhism at an early period as protectors and assistants. These new Buddhist gods include the previous human Buddhas, the Dhyāni Buddhas of the Four Quarters (later so prominent in Chinese Buddhism), their spiritual sons, the Bodhisattvas (of whom Maitreya alone was known to the Hīnayāna), and ultimately the feminine divinities (Tārās) associated with the latter and as saviouresses ranking with them. Additional to these are the many deified spells and mantrams; and the deities already mentioned are multiplied indefinitely by the recognition of an infinite variety of forms, peaceful and militant.

Thus we are prepared for the development of the succeeding centuries, when Indian genius, impelled by the necessity of service of the devotional cults, created an iconography adequate to the portrayal of all those spiritual and physical powers and forces which are deified in the Hindu and Buddhist pantheons.

CHAPTER NINE

KUṢĀṆA AND LATER ĀNDHRA PERIOD

BEFORE describing the actual art of the Kuṣāṇa and later Āndhra periods in India proper, we must consider the great production of Buddhist sculpture associated with the monuments and monasteries of Taxila, and of the Gandhāra provinces of the North-West Frontier. These sculptures date for the most part between A.D. 50 and 300; in even the earliest the type is already fixed. The themes without exception are Indian Buddhist. The Buddha figure occurs abundantly both as the central figure of historical compositions and in separate seated and standing images: the ancient symbolic formulae are very rarely seen. Forms and composition of Western (provincial Hellenistic) origin are everywhere conspicuous in Gandhāra art, side by side with other elements of Indian origin. The quality of the art is effeminate and sensual, its intention realistic. It appears to be the work of craftsmen of foreign origin or descent, familiar with late Greek models, adapting their stock motifs to the requirements of Buddhist patrons, the Indo-Scythian and Kuṣāṇa kings of the North-West : there is nothing to suggest that Indian artists from the plains had any part in it. On the contrary, Gandhāra art exerted a considerable influence on the contemporary school at Mathurā, and to a less degree elsewhere in India proper, even extending to the South. But we must not misunderstand the nature of this influence. The genius of Hellenistic art is foreign to Indian psychology. Western art at all times tends to representation, Indian to symbolism: the influence of Gandhāra, hardly recognizable after A.D. 300, constitutes an episode, and not a stage in a continuous development.

We must pause, however, to consider at greater length the origin of the Buddha image. It has been argued from the Gandhāra Buddhas of the Apollo type that the Buddha image is of Greek origin and first came into being at Gandhāra. There do not exist, either in Gandhāra or in India proper, Buddha image known to be earlier than the first century A.D. In both areas they appear simultaneously, in Hellenistic types at Gandhāra, and in the tradition of ancient Indian art at Mathurā. It is agreed that the earliest Gandhāra figures are 'already stereotyped' and that Buddha figures must have been made as early as the first century B.C. Were then these prototypes of Hellenistic or of Indian origin? We shall tabulate the arguments for either view and leave the question undecided.

For the Greek origin:

(1) It is admitted that Buddhist figures in Gandhāra are adaptations of Western types. A certain amount of originality, or rather novelty, is proved by the occurrence of such types as those of the realistic emaciated Buddhas, which have no part even in later Indian Buddhist art. Early Indian religious art, on the other hand, makes use of primal symbols without anthropomorphic icons.

(2) The admitted fact that formulae of Hellenistic art are adopted to a greater or less extent in India proper, and can be recognized in Indian art for several centuries. Moreover, such phenomena are not altogether new: Western (Iranian rather than Greek) motifs are already to be recognized in Early Buddhist art and are conspicuous in the court art of Asoka and in decorative motifs.

(3) As no Indian Buddha figure older than the Gandhāra sculptures is certainly known, it is at least possible that the first Buddha images were made in Gandhāra, and formed the models of later Indian Buddhist art. (The apocryphal legends in Buddhist literature cannot be accepted as evidence that images of the Buddha were made already in the fifth century B.C.)

For the Indian origin:

(1) The purely Indian attitudes of the Gandhāra figures, the use of the lotus seat, often awkwardly represented, the characteristically realistic transformation of the *uṣṇīṣa* (which appears already in Indian art at Bodh Gayā) would seem to imply the existence of purely Indian prototypes.

(2) Bodhisattva and Buddha figures of the first century A.D. do actually occur at Mathurā, in a style quite distinct from that of Gandhāra, and plainly developed from earlier Indian art, also, a little later, at Mīrpur Khās in Sind.

(3) Negative evidence holds good as much in one sense as the other, particularly in a period of still uncertain chronology.

(4) The *yogi* seated beneath a tree, in *padmāsana,* 'gazing upon the end of his nose', in profound meditation, was then, as now, a familiar spectacle. Once the need of an image had been felt (and we have recognized the sources of such a need in the general development of Indian religious experience), the choice of the meditating or teaching *yogi* figure must have been inevitable. What other form *could* have been appropriately set beneath the *bodhi* tree, which had hitherto stood alone as the sign of the Great Enlightenment? It is certain that no Western prototype of a seated figure with crossed legs and hands in *dhyāna* or *bhūmi-sparśa mudrā* can be cited or imagined.

(5) Regarded simply as works of art, there is no suggestion of primitive inspiration in Gandhāra sculpture. In other cycles of art, creative energy finds immediate expression in powerful and simple forms. Are we to consider Gandhāra a case unique in the history of art?

It will be seen from these considerations that it may be regarded both as *a priori* likely and as historically possible, that the Buddha image wherever found is based on Indian prototypes: just as the images of Bodhisattvas and those of Hindu deities are derived in direct descent from Indian sources.

The most important remains of Buddhist sculpture of the Kuṣāṇa period are those of Mathurā, Amarāvatī and Ceylon. The former, now for the most part in the Mathurā Museum, include the oldest Buddha figure so designated in an inscription. As this seated Buddha, from Aṇyor, is headless, we have reproduced (Fig. 17) the inscribed Katrā Bodhisattva, the pose and general appearance of which are identical with those of the Aṇyor Buddha. It will be observed that the right hand is raised in *abhaya mudrā,* the left hand rests on the thigh, the elbow being raised: this position of the left arm scarcely recurs in Indian art, but survives or reappears in a characteristic seated pose of Javanese actors. Another Buddha, of the same school and period, the robe in this case covering both shoulders, is shown in Fig. 18. It will be remarked that these images are far more energetic than those of the Gandhāra school, and belong to the old tradition of Bhārhut and pre-Mauryan sculpture.

Very remarkable are the Bacchanalian groups of Mathurā, perhaps representing Kuvera, and in any case connected with Yakṣa cults absorbed into popular Buddhism. Figures of Yakṣas and Nāgas, both in the round and as reliefs on railing pillars, are commonly found. The Nāga cult seems to have flourished at Mathurā, and it is noteworthy that the later images of Balarāma are identical with and no doubt derived from these Nāga types.

Mathurā has also yielded a number of inscribed funerary (?) statues of Kuṣāṇa kings (Kaṇiṣka, Fig. 19); these show no signs of Hellenistic influences, though the costume, like that of the Kuṣāṇa kings on the coins, a coat with long skirts, and high boots, is rather central Asian (Yueh Chi) than Indian.

Buddhist sculptures of the Mathurā school have been found at Sārnāth and Saheṭh Maheṭh (Śrāvastī), the latter a part of a Bodhisattva figure, with an inscription, probably older than the Aṇyor Buddha, and before Kaṇiṣka. The standing Bodhisattva in the Calcutta Museum is a massive and realistic figure of the old Indian type. The Buddhist sculpture of Peshawar and Taxila in the time of Kaṇiṣka, in the inscribed 'Kaṇiṣka casket' with seated Buddha figures, is altogether in the Greco-Buddhist or Indo-Hellenistic style of the North-West. We have not described these works in detail, as they fall without the central tradition and direct evolution of Indian art.

A Jaina *stūpa* has been excavated at Mathurā and has yielded many railing pillars decorated with nude Yakṣīs associated with trees, the woman and tree motif which recurs so constantly in Indian art from the Bhārhut period onwards. A 'tablet of homage' with a relief of a Jaina stūpa shows that the Jaina monuments were identical in form with the Buddhist.

Coins of the period are interesting, both for their improved technique and for the variety of subjects represented. Two-armed figures of Śiva have already appeared on the coins of the Parthian Gondophares and the Great Yueh Chi; those of Kaṇiṣka show the deity sometimes with two, sometimes with four arms. The Kaṇiṣka coins bear representations of a varied assemblage of Zoroastrian, Greek, Mithraic and Indian deities: Buddha is represented standing in a costume of Greek aspect and seated in Indian fashion. Remains of Hindu sculptures of the Mathurā school will no doubt be recognized when the sculptures are studied in greater detail from this point of view. A three-headed Kuṣāṇa sculpture, for example, in the Mathurā Museum still awaits identification. The oldest known Brāhmaṇical temple, of the first century B.C. or A.D. and adorned with Śaiva reliefs, exists at Ramnagar in the Bareli district. The oldest Sanskrit inscription occurs on the sacrificial posts of Isapur.

Contemporary with the Kuṣāṇa sculpture of Northern India is the Buddhist art of the later Āndhra dynasty of the Deccan, best known by the remains of the magnificent *stūpa* of Amarāvatī. The original *caitya* dates from about 200 B.C. and some reliefs are of the first or second century B.C.: the casing slabs and the great railing, and also the few Buddha figures, date from the latter part of the second century A.D. or at any rate not later than A.D. 250. The railing is the most elaborate known of its kind; about six hundred feet in circumference, it stood some thirteen or fourteen feet above the pavement level. As usual, it consisted of pillars connected by crossbars, standing on a plinth. Each upright was decorated with full and half lotus rosettes, infinitely varied in treatment, and with reliefs in the intervening spaces. Each crossbar bore another full lotus rosette on each side. The coping and plinth were elaborately ornamented, the former with a long undulating garland carried by men, the latter with boys and animals. The casing slabs for the most part represent scenes from the life of Buddha treated in accordance with the old tradition in which the Buddha figure is omitted. It is estimated that a total surface of nearly seventeen thousand square feet was covered with sculptured reliefs: it is very possible that these were originally covered with a thin coat of fine plaster and painted.

The sculpture is very vigorous and full of movement, sometimes passionately devotional (Fig. 21), sometimes humorous, always voluptuous and decorative. The whole is a masterpiece of pure design, charming in every detail.

On the other hand, the Buddha figure is still intensely ascetic and severe, representing pure thought rather than design; sculpture in the round is not yet perfectly absorbed by or attuned to the rhythm of the social order, but has a slower tempo and more restricted scope. The Amarāvatī and Siṅhalese Buddhas and Bodhisattvas of the second and third century A.D. are unsurpassed as pure sculpture; but it is only in the Gupta period that sculpture in the round, the cult figure, is perfectly assimilated to the ensemble of the architecture and reliefs, and shares their decorative qualities. We may put it that before the third century each image is an individual achievement, and iconography is not yet rigidly defined. It is only in the first century A.D. that deities are represented with four arms, and many-headed and many-armed forms are still later: about the second or third century the old Buddhist representation of the Nativity (Māyā Devī with the elephants) is being taken over into Hindu (Paurāṇic) iconography as Gajalakṣmī, while the development of Gaṇeśa from Jambhala (the mongoose of the latter becoming the rat of the former) may be still later. The compilation of the earlier *Śilpaśāstras* may be dated in a general way as late Kuṣāṇa or early Gupta, the *dhyāna mantras* of personal worship becoming the *sādhanās* of the imagers' handbooks: thereafter, image-making becomes a craft inseparable from architecture and all other crafts.

The earliest of the innumerable references to painting in Indian literature, occurring in the epics and early Buddhist texts, bespeak a highly developed art: paintings on cloth, on wooden panels, and on walls, and the painted halls of royal palaces are mentioned. To Buddhist monks the representation of the human figure was forbidden, and only that of wreaths and creepers permitted. How soon this rule was neglected may be seen not only from the literature, but also in the paintings of cave temples Nos. IX and X at Ajaṇṭā, ranging from 100 B.C. to A.D. 200. Here there are representations of Jātaka scenes, and of seated and standing Buddhas. The fine example of a standing King or Yakṣa reproduced by Professor S. Taki in the *Kokka*, No. 355, closely parallels the sculptures of Bhārhut and Sāñcī, and the early work of the Mathurā school. Like the sculpture, the painting is static and enormously dignified, rather than elegant or facile. Technically it is far advanced, the face and figure being shown in three-quarter profile with thorough understanding of the problems involved; the draughtsmanship is able and unhesitating, but quite without the bravura and the sweetness of Ajaṇṭā painting of the Gupta period. The Buddha figures in the same caves are not likely to be earlier than the second century A.D. The poorly preserved and much restored frescoes of the Jogimāra cave in the Rāmgarh hill (Orissa) are probably of the first century B.C., possibly somewhat earlier: seated and standing figures and *caitya* halls, and decorative work with *makaras* and other marine monsters are represented, but the whole is too badly effaced to admit of exact identification.

SELECT BIBLIOGRAPHY

Banerji, R.D. : *Three Sculptures in the Lucknow Museum.* Archaeological Survey of India, Annual Report, 1909-10, Calcutta, 1914.

Burgess, J. : *The Buddhist Stupas of Amaravati and Jagayyapeta.* London, 1887.

Notes on the Amaravatī Stupa. Madras, 1892.

Gandhara Sculptures, Journal of Indian Art, Vol. 8. London, 1898-1900.

Foucher, A. : *L'art greco-bouddhique du Gandhara,* 2 Vols. Paris, 1905, 1918.

Macdonell, A.A. : *The Development of Early Hindu Iconography.* In *Festschrift Ernst Windisch.* Leipzig, 1914.

Marshall, J.H. : *Guide to Taxila.* Calcutta.

Parker, H. : *Ancient Ceylon.* London, 1909.

Rea, A. : *South Indian Buddhist Antiquities.* Madras, 1894.

Smith, V.A. : *The Jain Stupa and other Antiquities of Mathura.* Allahabad, 1901.

Spooner, D.B. : *Excavations at Shāh-jī-kī-Dherī,* Archaeological Survey of India, Annual Report, 1908-9. Calcutta, 1912.

Excavations at Sahri-Bahlol, Archaeological Survey of India, Annual Report, 1909-10. Calcutta, 1914.

The Kanishka Casket Inscriptions, Archaeological Survey of India, Annual

Report, 1909-10. Calcutta, 1914.

Vogel, J. Ph. : *Nāga Worship in Ancient Mathurā,* Archaeological Survey of India, Annual Report, 1908-9. Calcutta, 1912.

Inscribed Gandhara Sculptures, Archaeological Survey of India, Annual Report, 1903-4. Calcutta, 1906.

Catalogue of the Archaeological Museum at Mathurā. Allahabad, 1910.

The Mathurā School of Sculpture, Archaeological Survey of India, Annual Report, 1906-7 and 1909-10, Calcutta, 1909 and 1914.

Excavations at Saheth-Maheth, Archaeological Survey of India, Annual Reports, 1907-8. Calcutta, 1911.

Explorations at Mathura, Archaeological Survey of India, Annual Report, 1911-12. Calcutta, 1915.

CHAPTER TEN

THE GUPTA PERIOD

THE Gupta period is the golden age of India, the age of maturity when Bharatavarṣa attained the fruit of her birth. Political power and abundant wealth inevitably provide the physical medium for that unique mastery of life which marks the culmination of Indian civilization. The combination of brilliant intellectual and spiritual development with the utmost sensuousness of experience and expression more than justify the Indian tradition of the court of Vikramāditya. Close relations with the West by way of Bactria in the North and the Roman trade in the South have now been broken: India's foreign relations are now, and for a thousand years to follow, with the Far East by way of Central Asia, and with Further India and Indonesia by sea. It is under Indian influence that the Unity of Asia (a unity to which the later culture of Islam is foreign) came into being.

India herself is now for the first time spiritually and intellectually one, the normal rhythm of life is established in and by the epics, and a fundamental unity of experience and character transcends all political, racial, linguistic and sectarian distinctions. Vedic ritualism, a survival from a remote past, and primitive Buddhism, correctly interpreted by mediaeval Hindu thought as a kind of heresy or treason against the social order, are no longer state religions: Vaiṣṇavism, Śaivism, Śāktism and Mahāyāna Buddhism, the religions of devotion to Viṣṇu, Śiva, Devī, Buddha or Bodhisattva, are patronised impartially. Images and temples appropriate to each of these persuasions of Hinduism appear in profusion, and determine the leading forms of all later imagery and architecture. Iconography and the theory of music and dancing are codified. In the art of the Gupta period all earlier tendencies converge: an identical quality appears not only in art of diverse sectarian application, but in the art of every province, from the Himālayas to Ceylon. We no longer meet with primitive qualities or *naïveté* in Indian art—its character is self-possessed, urbane, at once exuberant and formal. All foreign influences have been absorbed and Indianised. There is no divergence of feeling between doctrine and expression—it has come to be understood that the forms and experiences of finite life are revelations of the infinite: in this age, we can truly say that the five senses are the chief inlets of the soul. Philosophy and faith possess a common language in this art that is at once abstract and sensuous, reserved and passionate.

Buddhism is now completely fused with the national life; the Buddha figure, still extraneous at Amarāvatī, has become an integral part of the architecture. The paintings of Ajaṇṭā reflect the same abundant, exquisite, sophisticated and brilliant life that forms the theme of Bāṇa's *Kādambarī*. This was an age which could afford to permit to itself the fullest possible enjoyment of life, by right of innate virtue. In this connection it is worthwhile to remark that now for the first and only time in Indian history we meet with a practice of the arts as a personal achievement, side by side with the vocational and hieratic production. Individual men of letters—the 'nine gems of Vikramāditya's court'—who are not by immediate profession religious teachers, attain to fame; painting is an accomplishment of kings and queens (portrait painting is a common device of the classical drama); and there are indications here, and in the erotic literature, that secular painting was regarded, like music and poetry, as a source of the experience of *rasa*.[44] Samudragupta's musical skill is commemorated in the gold coins where

44 The *Uttararāmacarita* of Bhavabhūti, I, 39, speaks of the queen receiving a latent impression (*bhāvanā*) by looking at the pictures. Vātsyāyana's *Kāmasūtra*, a compilation of older material, perhaps made in the early Gupta period, mentions painting as one of the sixty-four arts belonging to an elegant education. Yaśodhara's later commentary enumerates the Six Limbs (*Ṣaḍaṅga*) of painting as follows:

Rūpabheda, distinction of forms (i.e., knowledge of the *lakṣaṇas* of persons to be represented).

(Continued on next page)

he is represented as playing the vīṇā. The great excellence of the Gupta coinage must be attributed to the cultivated taste of the kings. But these personal achievements should scarcely be regarded, like those of a modern genius, as aberrations from life or the exploitation of a personality: they are the ornaments and pinnacles of the structure of the race, perfectly in harmony with all its architecture.

Earlier Indian art is, so to speak, a product of nature, rather than of artifice, and characterised by naturalism and simplicity. Gupta art is the flower of an established tradition, a polished and perfected medium, like the Sanskrit language, for the statement of thought and feeling: and having thus become an ordered language with a grammar and vocabulary of its own, its forms are by hypothesis conventioned ('agreed upon') and ideal—its truth of utterance does not depend upon, though it may include, a visual resemblance to natural forms.

We shall now refer to the most important surviving monuments of the period. At Bhītargāon there exists an ancient brick temple, square in plan with a high tower, probably of the sixth century; it is decorated with carved brickwork and brilliant terracotta panels of Śaiva themes. There are cave temples at Udayagiri near Besnagar in Bhopal, one of which bears an inscription dated equivalent to A.D. 401. Here the principal sculptures are the great relief façade representing the Raising of Earth from the waters by Viṣṇu as Varāha, a Paurāṇic subject, and the representation of river goddesses, common in Gupta art, in the Candragupta cave. A large relief at Paṭhārī, also in

Pramāṇa, proportion (i.e., knowledge of the canons of proportion, *tālamāna*).

Bhāva, mood, technically the rise of emotion in a mind previously at rest, here the corresponding quality in a work of art.

Lāvaṇya-yojanam, infusion of saltness (*lāvaṇya*, in a human being means beauty, charm, grace, allure, here the like quality in painting).

Sādṛśya, likeness (perhaps with reference to portraiture).

Varṇikābhaṅga, distribution of pigments (i.e., knowledge of the colours proper to each subject).

Yaśodhara adds, 'These arts avail to awaken passion in others and for pastime.'

Bhopal, represents the nativity of Kṛṣṇa. The temple of Deogarh in Jhānsi District (sixth century) has relief panels of Vaiṣṇava subjects, including the Birth of Brahmā and the salvation of the King of Elephants, a theme that recurs much later in Rajput painting. Fragmentary sculptures of the fourth century at Maṇḍor near Jodhpur show scenes from the Kṛṣṇa *enfances*, including the raising of Mt. Govardhana. The Calcutta Museum has a fine Śiva and Pārvatī group from Kosām near Allahabad, dated equivalent to A.D. 458-9. There is a three-headed Viṣṇu of the fifth or sixth century in the Boston Museum, and a four-headed copper or bronze image of Brahmā, of early Gupta date, from Mīrpur Khās, in the Museum at Karachi.

The Dancing Śiva type appears in the decoration of the Durgā temple at Aihole. This temple, of fifth century date, is remarkable for its apsidal plan; it is like a structural Buddhist church, with a Hindu shrine in place of the *stūpa*. Two old Buddhist churches, with apsidal plan and barrel roof respectively at Ter (the ancient Tagara, in Haidarabad) and Chezarla (Kistna district) have been converted to Vaiṣṇava and Śaiva uses and so preserved. A series of ancient temples at Aihole, Lāḍ Khān and Durgā temples, fifth century, Meguti and Huccimalliguḍi temples, sixth century, and others of the same period with fine Vaiṣṇava reliefs as ceiling panels are closely related to the excavated architectural forms of the neighbouring Bādāmi caves. The latter include Cave I, a Śaiva temple with a Tāṇḍava sculptured relief, Caves II and III which are Vaiṣṇava temples, and a Jaina cave, No. IV, with relief sculptures of the Jinas; the first three of the sixth century, the latter of the seventh. Caves XVI, XVII and XIX at Ajaṇṭā date from the close of the fifth century, Cave XXVI from about A.D. 600. Cave XIX has a very richly sculptured façade, with many Buddha figures. Related to this is the Viśvakarmā Buddhist cave at Ellora, of the sixth or early seventh century, where, as at Ajaṇṭā, the front of the *stūpa* is occupied by an immense Buddha, in this case seated, with two attendants. At Sārnāth, the Dhāmekh *stūpa* and a richly carved lintel with Jātaka subjects illustrate the wealth of architectural remains, while the site has also yielded many well-preserved Buddha figures. The Buddhist temple at Buddha Gayā, founded by Aśoka, dates in the main from the sixth century, with restorations up to the twelfth, and modern restorations. A Bodhisattva torso from Sāñcī in the Victoria and Albert Museum, London, is amongst the finest surviving examples of late Kuṣāṇa or early Gupta art. The great standing Buddha (Fig. 25) at Mathurā (fifth century) is even more impressive: the beautifully decorated *śiraścakra* is typical of the Gupta style, and contrasts with the plainer types of the Kuṣāṇa period. Many fine Buddhist bronzes have been found at Buddhapāḍ in the Bezwada district: a seated Buddha of similar character from Badullā is now in the Colombo Museum, and a standing image, said to have been found in Burma, is now in the Boston Museum. The finest of the stone sculptures of Anurādhapura already referred to (Figs. 22 and 24) are probably of late Kuṣāṇa, and many others are of early Gupta age. Of other Buddhist sculptures the most important are the Buddha and Bodhisattva figures from Mathurā (standing Buddha, Fig. 25), Sāñcī, and Sārnāth (amongst others the well-known torso in the Victoria and Albert Museum, London); the colossal copper statue of Buddha from Sultānganj, now in the Birmingham Museum, dating about A.D. 400 and weighing over a ton; the seated Buddha of Maṅkuwār, dated equivalent to A.D. 446-8, with webbed hands; and the Kāṅgṛā brass Buddha of the sixth century, inlaid with silver and copper, now in the Lahore Museum. Remains of the Gupta period will no doubt be found at Nālandā as the excavation proceeds. The seals and gold coins of the Guptas are masterpieces of design, the coins superior to those of any other phase of Indian art. There is a small gold standing image of Buddha, of the Gupta age, in the British Museum. We must not omit a reference to the well-known Iron Pillar of Delhi, erected about A.D. 415 by Kumāragupta I.

The frescoes of Ajaṇṭā preserve an infinitely precious record of the golden age of Indian painting. The greater part, excepting those in Caves IX and X already referred to, are to be dated between A.D. 550 and 642, those in Cave I being latest, and contemporaneous with the related paintings at Bāgh in Mālwā. This is the picture of a halcyon age, where renunciation and enjoyment are perfectly attuned, an art at once of utmost intimacy and reserve. Every gesture springs in godlike fashion directly from the natural dispositions of the mind: this is not the self-betrayal of innocence, but utterance in terms of a supreme courtesy—the language of gesture had already its lexicons, the analysis of feeling had been made in learned treatises. All this is comparable only with the virtue still to be recognized in Indian and Indonesian dancing and music, where learned form is the natural medium of expression of the deepest feeling. It is of no importance that we know nothing of the painters' names: all India was richly painted in these days, and the art is the art of a race and not of any individual. The subjects treated by Ajaṇṭā painters are those characteristic of Buddhist art at all times—scenes from the life of Buddha, and Jātakas. The following are amongst the most important compositions:

Cave I : Māra Dharṣaṇa, Great Bodhisattva (Fig. 28), 'Indra and Śacī', ceiling with love scenes, and 'Persian Embassy' (really a Bacchanalian Pañcika).

Cave II : Great Miracle at Śrāvastī, Kṣāntivādin Jātaka, Indraloka scenes, decorated ceiling.

Cave XVI : Buddha triad, Great Renunciation, Dying Princess. A fragment from this cave is in the Boston Museum.

Cave XVII : Seven Buddhas, Wheel of Causation, Mahāhaṁsa, Mātṛpoṣaka, Ṣaḍḍanta, Sibi (with inscription), and Viśvantara Jātakas, Apsarases, decorated ceiling.

Contemporary with some of the Ajaṇṭā paintings are the similar (fifth century) frescoes in a rock pocket at the Sīgiriya fortress in Ceylon, representing Apsarases (the lower part of the body in each case is concealed by clouds, indicating that celestial beings are intended) in the likeness of princesses accompanied by maid-servants carrying trays of flowers. Jaina paintings, evidently of great importance and beauty, have been recently discovered at Śittanavāśal near Pudukottai, and assigned by M. Jouveau-Dubreuil to the time of Mahendravarman I (600-25).

SELECT BIBLIOGRAPHY

Allan, J.: *Catalogue of the Coins of the Gupta Dynasties . . . (in the British Museum)*. London, 1914.

Bāṇa: *Kādambarī,* translated by C.M. Ridding. London, 1905.

Harṣacarita, translated by E.B. Cowell and F.W. Thomas. London, 1897.

Bhandarkar, D.R.: *Two Sculptures at Maṇḍor,* Archaeological Survey of India, Annual Reports, 1905-6. Calcutta, 1909.

The Temples of Asia, Archaeological Survey of India, Annual Report, 1908-9. Calcutta, 1912.

Burgess, J.: *Notes on the Buddha Rock-temples of Ajanta.* Bombay, 1879.

Cousins, H.: *Ancient Temples of Aihole,* Archaeological Survey of India, Annual Report, 1907-8. Calcutta, 1911.

Buddhist Stūpa at Mīrpur Khās, Archaeological Survey of India, Annual Report, 1909-10. Calcutta, 1914.

Golobrew, V.: *Peintures bouddhiques aux Indes, Annales du Musée Guimet,* 40. Paris, 1914.

Griffiths, J.: *The Paintings in the Buddhist Cave Temples of Ajanta,* 2 Vols. London, 1896-7.

The Ajanta Cave Paintings, Journal of Indian Art. London, 1900.

Herringham, C.: *Ajanta Frescoes,* 2 Vols. India Society, London, 1915.

Jouveau-Dubreuil: *The Pallava Paintings.* Hindustan Review, May, 1922. (Originally printed as a broadside, with one illustration, Pudukottai, 1920.)

Marshall, J.H. and Sahni, D.R.: *Excavations at Maṇḍor,* Archaeological Survey of India, Annual Report, 1909-10. Calcutta, 1914.

Smith, V.A.: *Catalogue of the Coins in the Indian Museum, Calcutta.* Oxford, 1906.

Indian Sculpture of the Gupta Period, A.D. 300-650. Ostasiatische Zeitschrift. Vol. III, 1915.

CHAPTER ELEVEN

EARLY MEDIAEVAL PERIOD

THE period following the Gupta and covering the transition from ancient to mediaeval India is one of even more abundant and elaborate production. The themes to be represented are more varied, in accordance with the full development of the mythology and cosmology, Hindu, Buddhist and Jaina. A technique had now been evolved and well established, fully adequate not only to the representation of the various Paurānic legends but to express the multifarious concepts of a very intricate theology. The imager had at his command not only craft traditions, but formulae (*sādhanās, dhyāna mantras,* etc.) proper to all the diverse aspects and manifestations of the One Supreme Power who takes the forms imagined by his worshippers and appropriate to their needs.

Early mediaeval sculpture has great dramatic force and freer movement than in the Gupta period. The national taste (the broad shoulders and the lion waist of the hero, the heroine's heavy breasts and so forth) is fully conscious and determines the character of works of which the details are ritually prescribed: there is a tendency to an increasing elegance and slenderness of form. The types of mediaeval architecture seem to spring into being suddenly, because the earlier development through wooden prototypes has inevitably been lost. Everywhere, too, there must have been painted walls, external and internal, of which no trace could be preserved. Were it possible to put back the hands of the clock and revisit ancient India, it is perhaps to the eighth century that we should turn, choosing for our pilgrimage a moment when temple-building and sculpture were in the fullest tide of their activity, and but little of the work of former centuries had yet been destroyed. As it is, the monuments of the eighth century, particularly those of Ellora, Elephanta and Mahābalipuram are better known to modern students than any others, and some, not without reason, have regarded this period as representing the zenith of Indian art.

At Ellora, the most renowned monument is the Kailāsa. This great shrine is not an interior excavation, like the earlier cave temple, but a model of a structural temple, cut from the living rock and standing free from it, though sunk, as it were, in the sloping side of the hill from which it has been excavated. Here the type of South Indian (Dravidian) architecture, with its flat roofs, enormous curved eaves, and domed *vimāna* or *śikhara* is fully developed. The main temple and most of its chapels are Śaiva. The best known relief (Fig. 29) represents Śiva and Pārvatī upon Mt. Kailāsa, Rāvaṇa below attempting to shake the mass from within, Śiva steadying it with the pressure of his foot—a magnificent dramatisation of the forces of strain and resistance at work in the earth's crust (we must not forget that Indian mythology is as much a natural philosophy as an art). On the north wall of the excavation is a shrine devoted to the three river goddesses, with colossal reliefs of Gaṅgā, Sarasvatī and Yamunā. A powerful relief, occupying an angle of the outer wall, represents Śiva destroying the triple city of the Asuras: a relief in the Laṅkeṣvara section, perhaps a century later, represents a six-armed dancing Śiva. Traces of painting can be seen on the roof of the main temple, which must be dated about A.D. 775. The Daśāvatāra cave, on the same hill slope, may be dated about 700: it contains some important and powerful reliefs, of which perhaps the finest represents the death of Hiraṇyakaśipu, where Viṣṇu appears in man-lion form, emerging from a pillar to lay a fatal hand upon the shoulder of the impious king who had denied his omnipresence.

The excavated Śaiva temples at Elephanta, near Bombay, preserve, besides many other sculptures of great importance, the well-known colossal 'Trimurti' (Maheśvaramūrti); a relief representing the marriage of Śiva and Pārvatī; and a four-headed statue of Sadāśiva, in the round.

In the South, the most famous monuments of Pallava art consist of excavated shrines; imitated structural temples (*rathas*) cut in the living rock and known as the Seven Pagodas; the great relief composition known as Arjuna's Penance; and the slightly later structural 'Shore Temple', all at Mahābalipuram, a little south of Madras. Structural temples (Kailāsanātha and Vaikuṇṭha Perumal) of the seventh century are to be found at Kañcipuram (Conjeevaram).

The monuments at Mahābalipuram are assigned to Narasiṁhavarman I (*ca.* 625-650) : those of his predecessor Mahendravarman I (600-625) are all 'caves'. The earlier excavated shrines include the two in which are found the representations of Kṛṣṇa raising Mt. Govardhana, and the great Durgā-Mahiṣāsura and Viṣṇu-Anantaśāyin compositions, the latter illustrated in Figure 30; the later group consists of the seven pseudo-structural temples ('Seven Pagodas') in a pure Dravidian style, some preserving the design of ancient Buddhist Vihāras, and one with a curved roof preserving the form of bamboo architecture as it may still be seen in Eastern India. The structural 'Shore Temple' belongs to the time of Rājasiṁhavarman, or is at any rate not later than the ninth century.

In Orissa, mainly at Bhuvaneśvara, Purī and Konārak, the continuous development of the northern style of architecture with sloping-sided *śikhara* crowned by an *āmalaka* may be followed from the flat or nearly flat-roofed Paraśurāmeśvara temple of the seventh or eighth century onwards. Similar to the Paraśurāmeśvara temple is the great Pāpanātha temple at Paṭṭaḍakal, and a little earlier is the Hucchimalliguḍi temple at Aihole in the west.

In the north, in the Kāngṛā and Kulu valleys respectively are found the rock-cut temples of Masrūr, and the structural temples of Baijnāth and Bajaurā.

The famous and picturesque Sun temple at Mārtāṇḍ in Kashmir, with its pointed arches, belongs to the very different local Kashmir school (A.D. 600-1100), and preserves a Western (classical) appearance.

Isolated sculptures of early mediaeval date are comparatively few or little known. The school of Mathurā seems to have produced nothing after the sixth century. Of the Buddhist remains at Nālandā, Sārnāth, and other Magadha and Orissan sites, some must be older than A.D. 900, but little has been done towards their accurate classification. Buddhist bronzes from Ceylon (the well-known Avalokiteśvara and Jambhala in the Boston Museum) are undoubtedly of the eighth century, and in the style of the Ellora reliefs. The best illustration of the sculpture, however, is found in the reliefs at Ellora and Elephanta, already mentioned, and in the composition called Arjuna's Penance at Mahābalipuram. This covers a vertical rock surface about 96 by 43 feet in area, divided into two parts by a cleft. The key to the meaning of the composition is to be found in the shrine and *yogi* worshipper on the left of the cleft. Two interpretations have been offered. According to that implied in the popular name 'Arjuna's Penance', the emaciated *yogi* is Arjuna, who thus propitiated Śiva in the high Himālayas, in order to obtain the boon of the use of the miraculous arms of Indra. Śiva appeared in the form of a hunter, engaged Arjuna in combat (the *Kirātārjunīya*) and, after overcoming him, bestowed on him the weapons of Indra. According to another interpretation, the whole composition represents the Descent of Gaṅgā, in which case the *yogi* must be identified as Bhagīratha: the *nāga* figures occupying the cleft are cited in support of this suggestion; but it is hardly possible that water should ever have actually flowed from above, as the advocates of this theory have supposed. In any case, we have before us a magnificent representation of a cosmic event, acclaimed by all orders of beings, approaching the scene on either side. The effect is most impressive, and must have been more so when the reservoir below was filled with water. The representations of elephants, deer and other animals are masterpieces of sympathetic interpretation, and with these figures must be grouped the remarkable 'Monkey Family' which occurs as an isolated sculpture, some distance to the north.

SELECT BIBLIOGRAPHY

Coomaraswamy, A.K.: *Mahayana Buddhist Images from Ceylon and Java,* Journal of the Royal Asiatic Society, 1909.

Golobew, V.: *La Descente de Ganga sur Terre à Mahāvalipuran,* in Ars Asiatica, Vol. III, 1921.

Havell, E.B.: *The Zenith of Indian Art,* Ostasiatische Zeitschrift.

Jouveau-Dubreuil: *The Pallavas.* Pondecheng, 1907.

Vogel, J.Ph.: *Iconographical Notes on the Seven Pagodas,* Archaeological Survey of India, Annual Report, 1910-11.

The Temple of Mahādeva at Bajaurā Kulu, Archaeological Survey of India, Annual Report, 1909-10.

CHAPTER TWELVE

MEDIAEVAL SCULPTURE
(A.D. 850–1200)

THE course of Indian temple building and sculpture continues uninterruptedly until the end of the twelfth century in Northern, Western and Central India, to the end of the thirteenth century in Orissa and Ceylon, and up to the present day in Southern India. The crest of the wave which rose to its highest in the Gupta period and advanced serenely during the two succeeding centuries is now breaking into foam. We see an increasing complication, hightened emphasis and a superb technical accomplishment and patience that are apt to overreach their end as, for example, in many of the Hoysaḷa (Cālukya) temples of the Deccan, where, it may be noted, many figures are signed by the Kanarese artists, a thing practically unknown in earlier periods, when the artist's name is only mentioned when he himself is the donor. The lavish use of decorative detail, going hand in hand with an attenuation of the actual elements of design and of the figure, take the place of the essential richness of the Gupta period : the erotic sculptures of Konārak are not one half so voluptuous as the Gupta Buddhas, or even the reliefs at Elephanta and Mahābalipuram. But it is only by reference to what is past that we can speak in this fashion; if we accept, as we should accept, the mediaeval buildings and sculptures in and for themselves, and wholly in relation to their own environment, we cannot fail to recognize their charm and infinite variety, the marvellous skill which uses stone like metal and covers whole ceilings with wreaths of dancers (Fig. 35) or with frozen lace.

The great Liṅgarāja temple in Orissa has been called the finest example of a purely Hindu temple in India; it dates from the ninth or tenth century, with later additions. The great tower is imposing beyond words, and the sculptured detail full of beauty. The somewhat similar Jagannātha ('Juggernaut') temple at Purī, dating from the latter part of the eleventh century, has a world-wide celebrity through the annual car festival. The Black Pagoda at Konārak, nineteen miles north-east of Purī, is assigned to the middle of the thirteenth century, and now forms one of the most magnificent ruins in India. The temple was dedicated to the Sun, and closely connected with the cults of Viṣṇu. The main temple is in the form of a car (*ratha* or *vimāna*) borne on immense wheels drawn by horses. Much of the sculpture may be described as a detailed illustration of the *Kāmasāstra*. This rich external decoration reflects the life of the world and the energizing power of the Sun: within, as in the majority of Hindu temples, all is plain. Of the external decorations of the later Hindu temples generally, we may say that there is represented, offered and dedicated to the deity, all the forms of life and all the activities that constitute the universe through which he manifests, and by which he is known to us; and in such a dedication, essential to the religious life, the exclusion of any aspect of life, even on grounds of human convenience, would amount to a denial of God.

Next in interest to the Orissan temples are those of Khajurāho and Gwalior, Jaina, Vaiṣṇava and Śaiva, ranging from the tenth to the eleventh century. The Kandaria Mahādeva temple at Khajurāho is a most imposing pile: the external aspect very clearly reflects the interior construction, which rises step by step, and terminates in the immense *śikhara*, which is gracefully supported by smaller replicas of itself on its sloping sides. Here too there are remarkable erotic sculptures, and more beautiful than those of Konārak. At Gwalior the Caturbhuj temple dates from the ninth century, the Sās Bahu and Telikā Mandir temples from the tenth or eleventh. The latter has no *śikhara*, but has a barrel-vaulted roof with *caitya* windows at each end.

One of the most famous of all Indian buildings is the Śaiva temple at Somnāth, which was destroyed by Maḥmūd of Ghaznī about 1025 and rebuilt by Kumārapāla in 1168. Perhaps the most remarkable mediaeval temple groups of Western

India, however, are those of the Jainas, at Mt. Ābu, Girnār and Palitāna. All three sites are sacred hills, where an aggregate of temples forms a city of the gods, not used by men. Those of Mt. Ābu are justly famed for the delicacy and intricacy of their decorative sculpture: they are built entirely of white marble, transported from a distance of twenty or thirty miles and carried up a hill four thousand feet in height. The most notable temples are those built by Vimala in 1031 and by Tejapāla in 1230. Tejapāla's temple is even more elaborate: a detail from a domed ceiling, a band of dancers, is reproduced in Figure 35. The Girnār site, sacred to Neminātha, is a city of temples built on the ledge of a cliff some six hundred feet below the summit of the hill, mostly erected or restored in the fifteenth century. It will be observed, too, that at Ahmadabad and elsewhere in Gujarat there are many beautiful mosques, built by craftsmen of the Jaina tradition and hardly differing from Jaina work save in the omission of all sculptured figures.

The architecture of the Hoysaḷas has already been referred to. The style can best be seen in the Dharwar district. The Śaiva temple at Ittagi, the Someśvara and Trikūṭeśvara temples at Gadag and a group of old temples at Lakkundi near by are the oldest. In Mysore proper the most remarkable temples are found at Belūr (about 1117) and Haḷebīḍ, where temple building was stopped by the Mussalmans about 1310. The Hoysaḷeśvara temple at Haḷebīḍ is one of the most richly ornamented in all India: almost the entire field of Indian mythology is illustrated and the decorative motifs are superimposed in frieze upon frieze. It is incomplete, as work was stopped by the Mussalman invasion in 1311.

There scarcely exist intact remains of any of the Buddhist monasteries and temples erected at Sārnāth, Nālandā and elsewhere in Bihar, Bengal and Orissa during the mid-mediaeval period; but, on the other hand, the Buddhist and Hindu sculptures of the Pāla dynasty (740-1197) are abundant and well preserved. The Calcutta Museum has a large series and others may be seen at Sāñcī, Sārnāth and in the larger European and American museums. Usually in fine black slate, they are executed with great precision of detail and smoothness of surface, but without deep feeling. The usual subjects recur: in Buddhist art, scenes from the life of the Buddha (the Eight Great Miracles is a favourite subject) and representations of Bodhisattvas, Tārās, and other divinities; in Hindu art, a wide range of Śaiva and Vaiṣṇava images. The metal figures on the whole are superior to those in stone: those in the Bengal Sahitya Parishad collection in Calcutta, and those from Rangpur (partly in the Calcutta Museum) are of exceptional beauty, and so too a number of smaller Hindu bronzes now in the Boston Museum and the small Buddhist bronzes which have lately been found at Nālandā. The names of Dhīmān and his son Bitpālo are mentioned as those of famous master-founders of Varendra in the eighth and ninth centuries.

SELECT BIBLIOGRAPHY

Banerji, R.: *Descriptive List . . . Bangiya Sahitya Parishad.* 1911.

Gangoly, M.: *Orissa and her Remains: Ancient and Mediaeval.* Calcutta, 1912.

Schiefner, A.: *Taranatha's Geschichte des Buddhismus,* translated from Tibetan. St. Petersburg, 1869.

Spooner, D.B.: *Vishnu Images from Rangpur.* Archaeological Survey of India, Annual Report, 1911-12.

Vasu, Nagendranath: *Archaeological Survey of Mayurabhanja.* Calcutta, no date (1911?).

Articles by various authors in *Rūpam,* Journals of Bihar and Orissa Research Society, Varendra Research Society, and Annual Reports of the Archaeological Survey of India.

CHAPTER THIRTEEN

SOUTHERN INDIA

TENTH TO EIGHTEENTH CENTURY

IN southern India, the most important of the earlier mediaeval temples is the great Śaiva shrine at Tanjore, an imposing and consistently planned building, with a high pyramidal tower rising over the main shrine: it was in process of construction by Rājarāja Deva about the end of the tenth century. Remains of other Dravidian temples earlier than the middle of the fourteenth century are very few. By the middle of the thirteenth century, however, the style is fully evolved: its leading characteristics include the great gateways (*gopuram*), pillared halls (*kalyāṇa-maṇḍapam*), the recurved cornices, elaborate monolithic columns and column brackets of rearing horses or monsters (*yālis* or lions) and the great processional corridors. Most of the South Indian shrines, from 1350 to 1750, consist of an accumulation of erections about a small and inconspicuous central shrine of greater antiquity, the enormous gateways rising high above everything else, and giving their distinctive character to the great cathedral cities. Parts of the temple at Cidambaram, one of the most sacred of all Southern shrines and dedicated to Naṭarāja, are as old as the tenth or eleventh century, the Nṛtya-sabhā, or Dancing Hall, of thirty-six pillars about eight feet high, being the oldest and most beautiful element. The Pārvatī temple is of the fourteenth or fifteenth century, the great gates still later. There is an early (fourteenth century) *maṇḍapam* in the great temple at Vellūr. The greater part of the temples at Srīraṅgam, Tāḍpatri, Kumbakoṇam, Rāmeśvaram, etc., belong to the sixteenth and seventeenth centuries.

The ruins at Hampi must be specially mentioned. Hampi, or Vijayanagar, was founded in 1336, attained its zenith under Kṛṣṇa Deva Rāya (1509-1530), and was sacked and destroyed in 1565. Kṛṣṇa Deva Rāya, to whom the beauty of the city was mainly due, was a veteran soldier and a polished gentleman and a patron of literature: with his two queens, he is worthily commemorated in the beautiful brass figures of the Śrīnivasa Perumāl temple, Tirumalai, Tirupati. To him, and to his queens, is due the most splendid building in the city, the Viṭṭhala temple, the finest building of its kind in southern India, and, in the words of Fergusson, marking the extreme limit in florid magnificence to which the (Dravidian) style advanced. The Kaḍailaikallu temple (Gaṇeśa), on the other hand, has plain stone walls and a flat roof line, which lend a peculiar dignity to the pillared *maṇḍapam* before it. There is also an important group of Jaina temples and several remarkable monolithic Brāhmaṇical sculptures (Narasiṁha, Gaṇeśa).

The great temple of Sundareśvara and Mīnākṣī at Madura is to modern travellers the best known of the Dravidian temples: it is mainly due to Tirumalai Nāyyak (1623-1659). The most remarkable buildings are the Vasanta Maṇḍapam (Tirumalai's choultry) and the hall of a thousand columns (really nine hundred and eighty-five, the place of fifteen columns being occupied by the Sabhāpati shrine): the pillars of both are extremely elaborate, many having life-sized figures forming part of their mass. The choultry took twelve years to build, from 1623 to 1635.

It should be remarked that in the Madras Presidency and in Travancore the learned tradition of temple-building has been preserved to the present day. The craft traditions are carefully handed down by the Kammālars, or superior craftsmen, who claim an equality with Brāhmaṇas: these Kammālars and their confrères, the Navandanno of Ceylon, largely of South Indian origin, still possess and make use of Sanskrit manuscripts of the *Śilpaśāstra*, or vernacular equivalents. There are interesting Hindu temples of the twelfth and thirteenth centuries at Polonnāruva in Ceylon.

We have still to refer to the great southern school of bronze (actually copper or, more rarely, brass) founding. The roots of this tradition go back to Buddhist art in the South (Amarāvatī, Bezwada, Ceylon, etc.). The earliest reference to the installation of Brāhmaṇical metal images, however, seems to be that of the Tanjore temple inscriptions referring to figures of Śaiva saints set up by Rājarāja Deva (about 1014). Figures of the deity himself must have been made before this. But, though dancing figures of Śiva are found in the Durgā temple at Aihole in the Gupta period and a little later at Elephanta, etc., we do not find amongst the stone sculptures any exact prototype or equivalent of the Naṭarājas and other typical metal images, and it is to be inferred that the Dravidian school of founding, so far as Śaiva and Vaiṣṇava images are concerned, developed contemporaneously with the theology and hagiology which they reflect, i.e., about the ninth or tenth century. With the possible exception of the Belūr Naṭarāja, of which the date is read by some as equivalent to A.D. 910 (more likely, 1511), the oldest known southern bronzes appear to be those from the Śiva Devāles of Polonnāruva, now in the Colombo Museum; later examples are to be found in Boston, Paris, London, etc. These can only be dated by a sense of style: many relatively modern examples are of excellent workmanship. There are probably others older and perhaps finer still in temples or buried.

The majority of southern bronzes, as might be expected, are Śaiva. The Naṭarāja type in particular is very well known (Fig. 36). The significance of this *nṛttamūrti* has been often explained: it represents the cosmic activity (*Pañcakṛtya*, 'Five Actions') of Śiva, the drum in the right hand indicating creation, the fire in left, involution and the dance continuance—a magnificent conception of the Absolute in action (*vyakta*, 'manifested'), complementary to the *avyakta* (unmanifested) symbol of the *liṅgam*, which forms the *dhruva* (immovable) icon in most Śaiva temples. Other forms of Śiva commonly met with in metal images are the Bhikṣāṭana Mūrtis, Dakṣiṇā Mūrtis and the various Umāsahita Mūrtis in which he is associated with Devī as Umā, Pārvatī or Śiva-Kāmī. Of the Śaiva saints, Māṇikka Vasagar (Fig. 37), Sundara Mūrti Svāmi (Fig. 38), Appar Svāmi and Tirujñāna Sambandha Svāmi are represented by cult images, often of considerable importance, the finest examples being those in the Colombo Museum

(Figs. 37 and 38). Vaiṣṇava images are rather less frequent, but some fine examples are known (one in the Boston Museum): the forms include Viṣṇu and Lakṣmī, Rāma groups and dancing and other forms of the young Kṛṣṇa; and of the saints, Hanumān, Garuḍa, the Twelve Āḷvārs and Meikanda Deva. There is also an image of Sūrya in the Colombo Museum.

Of Dravidian painting, the only old example to which I can refer is the fine eight-armed Naṭarāja fresco of the Śiva temple at Ettamānūr in North Travancore; but no systematic search for paintings has been made in the older parts and on the more neglected surfaces of Travancore and other Southern temples. More modern wall paintings, though crude in execution, are, however, evidently survivals of an old tradition: some of these are executed on glass. The late eighteenth and early nineteenth century portraits of Tanjore represent in the main an offshoot of Mughal art.

SELECT BIBLIOGRAPHY

Ayyar, C.P.V.: *Town-planning in Ancient Dekkan*. Madras, 1915.

Coomaraswamy, A.K.: *Bronzes in the Colombo Museum*. Colombo, 1914; *The Dance of Siva*. New York, 1917.

Gangoly, O.C.: *South Indian Bronzes*. Calcutta, 1914.

India-Society: *Eleven Plates*. London, no date.

Jouveau-Dubreuil, G.: *Archaeologie du Sud de l'Inde*. Paris, 1914.

Longhurst, A.H.: *Hampi Ruins*. Madras, 1917.

Rodin, A., Coomaraswamy, A.K., Havell, E.B., and Golobew, V.: *Sculptures civaites*, Ars Asiatica, III. Paris, 1921.

Sewell, R.: *A Forgotten Empire (Vijayanagar)*. London, 1900.

CHAPTER FOURTEEN

FURTHER INDIA AND INDONESIA

THE aborigines of Southern Indo-China and the Indonesian islands belonged to the Negrito type which extends from Madagascar to Formosa, the Philippines and New Zealand. At the beginning of the Christian era, northern races of Yünnan and Tibet are moving southwards and establishing themselves in the Irawaddy, Menam and Mekong valleys: at the same time Indian influences are beginning to be felt. About the fourth and fifth centuries, rulers of south Indian origin are in power in Cambodia, Campā, Sumatra and Java. With the exception of Burma, the prevailing religion is Brāhmaṇical (Śaiva): there are also original ancestor cults reinforced and modified by Indian ideas. Hīnayāna Buddhism reaches Sumatra in the fifth and Java in the sixth century, and appears in Cambodia still later. The period of Buddhist expansion extends from about A.D. 400 to 800. The 'Primitive' and 'Cubic' architecture of this period (Prapatom in Siam, numerous scattered sites in Cambodia, the Mison group in Campā, the Dierig Plateau groups in Java) is markedly Indian in character and purest in form: the finest sculpture, too, though but little is known, dates from the same time. The term 'Cubic' alludes to a characteristic aspect of the architecture, recognizable alike in Cambodia, Campā and Java. There are analogies with the brick temples of the Gupta period and the early Pallava architecture of southern India.

There follows a 'Classical' period in which the various kingdoms attain to the height of their power and magnificence, and to which belong the most splendid monuments. Towards the end of this period the various languages and literatures take shape. Mahāyāna Buddhism becomes increasingly prominent, intimately associated and bound up with Śaivism, as in Nepal. Vaiṣṇava forms of Hinduism also appear more conspicuously.

At the same time the apotheosis of kings and the cult of divine royalty become more and more prominent, as a result of which, particularly in Cambodia and Java, we find many posthumous statues of kings made in the form of the deity whom they worshipped and now indistinguishable from the statues of actual deities. The limiting dates are naturally not quite the same in all the kingdoms but, broadly speaking, extend from A.D. 750 or 800 to A.D. 1100 or 1200. The great monuments include the Schwezigon and Ānanda pagodas of Pagān in Burma (late eleventh century); Angkor Thom, with the palace and Bayon temple (ninth century) and Angkor Wat (twelfth century) in Cambodia; the Dong Duong group in Campā (ninth century); Caṇḍi Kalāsan (A.D. 778); Mendut, Borobuḍur (late ninth century) and Caṇḍi Loro Jongrang group at Prambānam (about A.D. 900) in Java. The architecture is at once luxurious and refined, with all its surfaces very richly decorated. Specially to be mentioned are the gallery reliefs of *jātakas* and other Buddhist subjects at Borobuḍur (Fig. 33); the Angkor Thom palace terrace with the frieze of elephants and *garuḍa* caryatides and, in the same city, the great Bayon temple with its towers with four faces (representing a *mukhaliṅgam*) and gallery relief; the Angkor Wat, with its reliefs of dancers and long gallery reliefs of Brāhmaṇical mythological and epic subjects (Fig. 34); the Ānanda temple at Pagān, with its Buddhist reliefs and glazed tiles illustrating *jātakas*.

Following upon these four or five centuries of power and splendour comes a gradual political disintegration and aesthetic decadence. This is the consequence in part of the exhaustion of energic and natural resources, and in part of invasions during the thirteenth to fifteenth centuries. Northern races (Lao-Thai, etc.) are pushed by the Mongols further southwards into Indo-China, the Mongols themselves capture Pagān, the Siamese possess themselves of Western Cambodia and finally of almost the whole kingdom; the Annamites push southwards the Cams (whose civilization perished *in toto* before the eighteenth century); the Mussalmans are possessed of Malacca and make themselves masters of Sumatra and finally of Java. Cambodia, under Siamese domination, becomes a Hīnayāna Buddhist country; Burma has remained essentially Buddhist throughout; Bali alone preserves a mixture of Hinduism and Buddhism.

The earlier part of the period of decay is by no means, however, without important and beautiful monuments. Amongst these may be mentioned the Sajjanālaya-Sukhodaya group in Siam, and all the Siamese Buddhist sculpture of the Ayuthia period; monuments at Binh Dinh, the Cam capital from 1100 onwards; Caṇḍi Jago (1280) and sculptures of Singosāri (1220-1292), and of Majapahit (1294 to 15th century), with its *Rāmāyaṇa* reliefs in *wayang* style, leading to the still surviving Hindu art of Bali. No great monuments date, in any case, from later than the fourteenth century. Apart from the ancient monuments, it is primarily in the theatre (music and classical dances of Burma, Siam, Cambodia and, above all, Java) that the splendour and spiritual power of the old Indo-Chinese and Indonesian cultures can now be best understood. For the rest, just as in Ceylon, the ancient artistic traditions are only to be recognized and recovered in the form of the folk arts.

SELECT BIBLIOGRAPHY

Duroiselle, Ch.: *The Stone Sculptures on the Ananda Temple at Pagan,* Annual Report, Archaeological Survey of India, 1913-4. Calcutta, 1914.

Fournereau, L.: *Le Siam ancien.* Paris, 1908.

Les Ruines khmères, Cambodge et Siam. Paris.

Groslier, G.: *Danseuses cambodgiennes.* Paris, 1913.

Krom, N.J.: *Inleiding tot de Hindoe-Javaansche Kunst.* The Hague, 1920.

Krom, N.J., and Erp, T. van: *Beschrijving van Barabudur.* The Hague, 1920.

Lelyveld, Th. B. Van: *De Javaansche Danskunst.* The Hague, 1922.

Parmentier, H.: *Inventaire descriptif des Monuments Cams de l'Annam.* Paris, 1909, 1918.

Catalogue du Musée Khmér de Phnom Penh, Bulletin de l'École francaise d'Extréme-Orient, 1919.

Sculptures Cames Conservees à Hué, Bulletin de l'École frandaise d'Extrême-Orient, 1919.

L'art d'Indravarman, Bulletin de l'École française de l'Extrême-Orient, 1919.

Pleyte, C.M.: *Indonesian Art.* The Hague, 1901.

Seidenstücker, K. : *Die Buddha-Legende in den Skulpturen des Ananda-Tempels zu Pagan*. Jahrbuch Hamb. Wiss. Anst. XXXII, 1914. Hamburg, 1916.

Voretzsch, E.A. : *Über altbuddhistische Kunst in Siam,* Ostasiatische Zeitschrift, Vol. V, pp. 1-26 and Vol. VI, pp. 1-22, 1916-7.

Indian Art in Siam, Rūpam, No. 3, 1920.

With, K. : *Java: Brahmanische, Buddhistiche und eigenlebige Architektur und Plastik auf Java*. Leipzig, 1920.

Javanische Bronsen. In 'Studien zur Kunst Asiens und Europas Josef Stryzgowski'. Vienna, 1922.

CHAPTER FIFTEEN

MEDIAEVAL BUDDHIST PAINTING

THE continuity of Indian painting from the seventh to the sixteenth century is to be inferred from literary references and from the internal evidences of later works. A limited number of actual documents has, however, survived, fairly representing the Buddhist and, as we shall see later, also the Jaina tradition. Of Indian Buddhist manuscripts, we have two from Bengal, on palm leaf (Cambridge MSS. Add. 1464 and 1688), one with painted wooden covers and both with miniatures representing Buddhist divinities and scenes from the life of the Buddha. Quite similar in style are the better known Nepalese MSS., usually texts of the *Aṣṭasāhasrikā Prajñāpāramitā.* One at Cambridge (MSS. Add. 1643), one formerly in Calcutta (MS. A 15, contents now missing!), and another in the Vredenberg collection, Calcutta, dated A.D. 1090, the first two containing respectively eighty-five and thirty-seven miniatures: both are of the early eleventh century. A similar text, dated about A.D. 1136, is now in the Boston Museum: there are eighteen miniatures in the text, and the wooden covers are intact, painted with divinities, and scenes from the life of Buddha, in particular, the Nativity and Māra Dharṣaṇa, also a group of the Seven Previous Buddhas and Maitreya. Professor A. N. Tagore owns a slightly later example, of which the covers are painted with *Jātaka* scenes. All these are MSS. on palm leaf: the miniatures are not (as in Persian manuscripts) organically and decoratively associated with the script, but occupy spaces (*ālekhya-sthāna*) left by the scribe to be filled by the painter. Besides these manuscripts, there are some undoubtedly ancient (tenth century?) Nepalese or, at any rate, Indian paintings of Bodhisattvas found at Tun Huang in Western China, and the same site has yielded what is probably the oldest surviving Tibetan Buddhist Banner.

Taking these Buddhist paintings collectively, we must

observe first that they obviously represent a continuation of the older tradition. The composition (arrangement of the figures) and iconography remain unchanged. The scene, however, is much more crowded, and colour is stronger and more formal. The art is essentially ecclesiastical in quality, much less emotional and more purely decorative than before. The glowing colour and accomplished drawing lend to all these manuscript illustrations a high aesthetic interest, and their rarity, a great historical value. The tradition of manuscript illustration and temple banner painting has survived in Nepal and Tibet up to the present day: many works of the seventeenth and eighteenth centuries are of high merit. The later manuscripts are usually written on thick black paper.

In Ceylon, remains of frescoes illustrating *Jātakas* were discovered on the walls of the Mahā Demala Saya at Polonnāruva (I can hardly say 'are preserved,' as they have been left exposed to sun and rain for many years): these cannot be later than the thirteenth century. A smaller composition at Hindagala, near Kandy, has been regarded as of seventh century date, but seems to me much later (twelfth to fourteenth century). Rock paintings at the Ridī Vihāra may be old. As might be expected, the mediaeval Sinhalese paintings are intermediate in character between those of the Sīgiriya period and the formal decorative art of the eighteenth century still preserved on the walls of many *vihāras* restored by Kīrtti Śrī, notably at Degaldoruwa near Kandy. There are also illustrated Sinhalese Buddhist manuscripts of the eighteenth and early nineteenth centuries. A tradition of Buddhist painting has also flourished in Burma, Siam and Cambodia, and survives to the present day in Burma and Siam. A highly sensuous and beautiful school of Buddhist and Hindu painting, on walls, on cloth and in manuscripts, was flourishing in Bali in the eighteenth and nineteenth centuries and still survives.

SELECT BIBLIOGRAPHY

Bell, H.C.P.B. : *Archaeological Survey of Ceylon, Report for* 1909. Colombo, 1914.

Bendall, C. : *Catalogue of the Buddhist Sanskrit MSS. in the University Library, Cambridge.*

Coomaraswamy, A.K. : *Mediaeval Sinhalese Art.* Broad Campden, 1908.

Portfolio of Indian Art. Boston, 1923.

Foucher, A. : *L'Iconographie bouddhique de l'Inde,* 2 Vols. Paris, 1900, 1905.

Joseph, G.A. : *Ceylon Administration Report for* 1918. Colombo Museum.

Vredenberg, E. : *The Continuity of Pictorial Tradition in the Art of India, Rūpam,* No. 1, 1920.

CHAPTER SIXTEEN

JAINA PAINTING

THE tradition of Jaina painting is recovered in manuscripts of the thirteenth and subsequent centuries. The text most frequently illustrated is the *Kalpasūtra* of Bhadrabāhu, containing the lives of the Jinas, most of the space being devoted to Mahāvīra. There are also illustrated cosmologies and cosmological diagrams, and appended to the *Kalpasūtra* there is usually to be found the edifying tale of Kālikācārya. The oldest illustrated manuscript is on palm leaf and dated equivalent to A.D. 1237. It is preserved in the Patan *bhāṇḍār*. Several illustrated *Kalpasūtras* to the fifteenth century are known (British Museum, India Office, Berlin, Boston, and Nahar collection, Calcutta). The pictures take the form of square panels of the full height of the page, occupying spaces left for the purpose: only in very rare cases is the whole page used. The proper subject to be represented is often indicated by a marginal legend, sometimes by a diagrammatic marginal sketch, the former doubtless due to the scribe, the latter to the artist taking note of his instructions. The same subjects are repeated in the various manuscripts almost without variation: it is very evident that both in composition and style the pictures belong to an ancient and faithfully preserved tradition. In some manuscripts the prevailing ground colour is red, in others there is a ground of gold leaf, which is left uncoloured to represent flesh tints, elsewhere yellow. In the example illustrated (Fig. 39), representing the Tonsure of Mahāvīra, the ground colour is red: Mahāvīra is seated beneath his tree, in a rocky landscape, attended by the four-armed Indra who receives the royal robes and gives the monastic robes in return. Heavy clouds (in Indian culture, an auspicious sight) hang low on the high horizon, as in early Rajput paintings; and, as in Sinhalese Buddhist art, the vacant space is occupied by a lotus rosette.

This is an art of fine and nervous draughtsmanship, calligraphic, facile and restless, intellectual rather than emotional. The colouring is strong, but less essential than the drawing; the composition formal and traditionally fixed, with abundance of circumstantial detail, giving a valuable picture of mediaeval manners. The drawing of the figure is peculiar : angular forms are very characteristic, the nose is sharply pointed, the corners of the eyes extended, as in Indian poetry, to meet the ears, and the further eye in, *profil perdu*, projects beyond the facial outline. Mediaeval Indian art has nothing finer to show than the Jaina paintings: only the early Rajput pictures of *rāgas* and *rāgiṇīs* are of equal aesthetic rank.

SELECT BIBLIOGRAPHY

Bhandarkar, D.R. : *Jaina Iconography*. Archaeological Survey of India, Annual Report, 1905-6. Calcutta, 1909.

Coomaraswamy, A.K. : *Notes on Jaina Art*, Journal of Indian Art, No. 127, 1914.

Guerinot, A. : *Essai de Bibliographie Jaina*. Paris, 1906.

Hüttemann : *Miniaturen zum Jinacarita*. Baessler Archiv, 1913.

Kirfel, W. : *Cosmographie der Jaina*. Leipzig, 1921.

Nahar, P.C., and Ghosh : *Epitome of Jainism*. Calcutta, 1917.

CHAPTER SEVENTEEN

RAJPUT PAINTING

RAJPUT painting—the painting of Rajasthan and the Panjab Himalayas under Rajput patronage—constitutes the only considerable body of Hindu painting extant. Wall paintings of the seventeenth century are found at Bikanir, Palitāna, Udaipur, paintings of almost life size at Jaipur, and probably wall paintings at other places in Rajputana: most of the work, however, is executed on paper and is of comparatively small size. The known paintings cover a period extending roughly from the middle of the sixteenth century to the beginning of the nineteenth, about three hundred years : the tradition is now almost extinct.

The themes are mainly Paurāṇic, epic, lyrical (Kṛṣṇa legends and Nāyikās) and musical: there is also some portraiture. Illustrated books are almost unknown; but well-known stories (e.g., Naḷa and Damayantī, the *Devī Māhātmya* of the *Mārkaṇḍeya Purāṇa*, etc.) are illustrated by series of drawings, sometimes with inscribed texts. The paintings fall into two groups geographically, Rājasthānī and Pahāṛī: the Pahāṛī paintings again into two groups, the earlier Jammu type, and the later (eighteenth century) Kāṅgṛā school, developed under the patronage of Rājā Saṁsāra Chand.

The greatest interest attaches to the sixteenth and early seventeenth century Rājasthānī paintings, which are almost invariably sets of pictures illustrating *Rāgamālās,* poems describing the thirty-six, or sometimes more, musical modes, the *rāgas and rāgiṇīs.* The paintings, like the poems which they illustrate, represent situations of which the emotional colouring corresponds to the feeling or burden of the musical mode. The time of day or night, time of year and state of the weather appropriate to the mode are also indicated in the paintings. The compositions for particular modes are generally constant;

thus, Bhairavī is always represented by a group of women worshipping at a Śiva shrine, Āsāvarī by a female snake-charmer, Toḍi by a woman with a *vīṇā*, to the sound of which the wild deer are attracted, Deśākhya by an acrobatic performance, and so forth. The poem for the Madhu-mādhavī Raginī (Fig. 41) refers to the pleasant rumbling of the thunder in the monsoon clouds, presaging rain, exciting the peacocks and, in like manner, the princess who longs to rest again in her absent husband's arms. Illustrations in the same style to Bāramāsa poems are much rarer. The constancy of the compositions, as well as the character of the art, make it evident that we are recovering here, just as in the case of the illustrations to the Jaina manuscripts, the formulae of an old and well-established tradition. Amongst such formulae may be cited as examples, the manner of representing clouds, rain and lightning, the representation of hills as conical eminences usually built up of smaller elements, covered with flowers and grasses, and the manner of differentiating between day and night by a variation of the background, without change in the illumination. A first glance at these paintings will suffice to convince the observer that they belong, and could only belong, to a pure Indian tradition: they are totally unlike Persian art of any period.

The most remarkable quality is one of glowing colour, only to be compared with enamel, though the painting has actually a dead matte surface: pure reds, yellows and also pinks, greens and browns are relieved by pure whites and velvet blacks. Gold, the use of which is probably foreign to indigenous tradition, does not occur until later in the history of Rajput painting. There are large masses of plain colour, against which the buildings, trees and figures stand out with great substantiality: this colour by itself establishes the planes and forms. The composition is architectural, not, as in Jaina painting, calligraphic. The drawing has magnificent bravura, but is less essential than the colour: one cannot imagine these pictures without their colour. Just as in the contemporary literary vernaculars, where words are reduced to bare roots, so in these tertiary Prākrits of pictorial art, the drawing is not explicit, but entirely allusive; that is to say, it is made up of elements which have no unequivocal and unmistakable significance taken alone, but when associated in phrases lend themselves to a very vigorous expression. In later Rajput art, the importance and continuity of the outline are restored, with loss of force, but with greater sweetness and realism. What we may call the fragmentary style of the early Rajput drawing has survived, however, on the circular playing cards of Bikanir, to the present day.

The paintings of the Jammu district, dating from the seventeenth and eighteenth centuries, very often have their inscriptions in the Ṭākrī character peculiar to the Ḍogrā hills. The best known examples are the large *Rāmāyaṇa* pictures in the Boston and New York Museums, in size and composition very suggestive of wall paintings. The colouring is only less vivid than that of the early Rājāsthanī pictures: in the example illustrated (Fig. 42) the colour of the ground, extending almost to the top of the picture, is a strong red, the fortress of Laṅkā is golden. The other subjects met with are *rāgas* and *rāgiṇīs* (often different from those of Rajasthan), mythological and rhetorical subjects and portraits. Chambā paintings must be grouped with those of Jammu, though many Kāṅgṛā paintings are to be found in the Chambā collections. All the Pahāṛī schools are closely interrelated.

The Kāṅgṛā school is a term used with reference to the work done in the whole Kāṅgṛā valley and adjacent Panjab plains, and includes also the branch represented by Molā Rām of Gaṛhwāl. It includes an early group of comparatively few examples (Figs. 43, 44) of very sensitive and highly emotional work, with soft powdery colour; and a later and larger group of brush drawings and pictures of the school of Rājā Saṁsāra Chand (late eighteenth and early nineteenth centuries). Kāṅgṛā painting is widely different from that of Rajasthan and Jammu. Kṛṣṇa subjects predominate (the whole of the *Prem Sagar* may be said to be fully represented); the Eight Nāyikās, usually after the text of the *Rasikapriyā* of Keśava Dās, are a favourite theme and other rhetorical subjects illustrating the stages of Sṛṅgāra may be found; romances such as Nala and Damayantī and the *Hamīr Haṭh* are treated in detail; there are some naturalistic drawings of flowers and fruits, and some portraits, but no *Rāgamālās*. This is essentially an art of outline, and exceedingly exquisite as such. The colour, it is true, is tender and charming, particularly in examples like the well-known 'Hour of Cowdust' (Boston), but the drawing alone gives everything essential. The physical type is long-eyed rather than large-eyed, and the forms are willowy and slender. The outline is continuous and made with long strokes of the brush, as at Ajaṇṭā: compared with the early Rājasthānī paintings, the Kāṅgṛā drawing may be described as a highly inflected language. Kāṅgṛā draughtsmanship, indeed, becomes increasingly realistic and explicit, and it is evident that the artists have to a considerable extent studied from nature, and if they have evolved a formula, it is rather their own than directly inherited. Mughal influences are occasionally to be recognized, particularly in the representation of night scenes, in which dramatic effects of firelight or torchlight are sometimes presented, a method quite foreign to the pure Indian tradition. One can hardly exaggerate the charm of the Kāṅgṛā paintings, and this charm depends equally on the subjects, emotional and lyrical, and the dainty and accomplished expression.

An artist of the name of Molā Rām, descended from Rajput painters originally working at the Mughal court in the time of Shāh Jahān, produced many works in the Kāṅgṛā *qalm*, at Gaṛhwāl, flourishing from about 1760 to 1833. He must have visited Kāṅgṛā. Some of his works are signed.

The subject of Mughal painting lies outside the scope of the present volume. It will be convenient, however, to mention its leading characteristics. The princes of the Timuria house continued in India the practice of their ancestors in Turkestan, who had been enthusiastic patrons of poets, painters and calligraphers. These influences at first predominate in Mughal painting (the best part of which belongs to the reigns of Akbar, Jahangir, and Shāh Jahān), but the school soon assumes a character of its own, more vigorous than that of Persian painting, which was already in decadence under Shāh Abbās the Great. It should not be forgotten that two-thirds of the Mughal painters, as we can see by their names, were Hindus. Mughal art, like the Mughal emperors, gradually became a definitely Indian thing; not, however, at all like the Rajput paintings, but realistic in method and personal and historical in interests. It excels in portraiture; and authentic likenesses of all the great men of the time, including the Mughal emperors themselves, are still in existence. Later, and particularly in the eighteenth century, there is a much closer assimilation to Hindu art, so far as subject matter is concerned; but the *rāgiṇīs* and *nāyikās* are treated by Mughal painters as material for art and not in the Hindu way, in all seriousness and for their own sake. The Delhi miniatures on ivory of the nineteenth century are a decadent offshoot of the Mughal school.

SELECT BIBLIOGRAPHY

Coomaraswamy, A.K. : *Rajput Painting*. Oxford, 1914.

The Eight Nayakas, Journal of Indian Art, London.

Coomaraswamy, A.K., and Sen, A. : *Vidyapati*. London, 1915.

Mukandilal : *Some Notes on Molaram, Rūpam,* No. 8, October, 1921.

Sen, Dinesh Chandra : *History of Bengali Language and Literature*. Calcutta, 1911. (Orissan Book Covers.)

Shastri, H. : *The Hamir Hath, or The Obstinacy of Hamir,* Journal of Indian Art, London, 1916.

Vogel, J.Ph. : *Catalogue of the Bhuri Singh Museum at Chamba*. Calcutta, 1909.

CHAPTER EIGHTEEN

UNDERSTANDING INDIAN ART

WORKS of art have been thought of in two very different ways. According to the modern view the artist is a special or even abnormal kind of man, endowed with a peculiar emotional sensibility which enables him to see what we call beauty; moved by a mysterious aesthetic urge he produces paintings, sculpture, poetry or music. These are regarded as a spectacle for the eyes or a gratification for the ear; they can only be enjoyed by those who are called lovers of art and these are understood to be temperamentally related to the artist but without his technical ability. Other men are called workmen and make things which everyone needs for use; these workmen are expected to enjoy art, if they are able, only in their spare time.

In ideal art, the artist tries to improve upon nature. For the rest, the truth of the work of art is held to be its truth to an external world which we call nature, and expect the artist to observe. In this kind of art there is always a demand for novelty. The artist is an individual, expressing himself, and so it has become necessary to have books written about every artist individually, for since each makes use of an individual language, each requires explanation. Very often a biography is substituted for the explanation. Great importance is attached to what we call genius, and less to training. Art history is chiefly a matter of finding out the names of artists and considering their relation to one another. The work of art itself is an arrangement of colours or sounds, adjudged good or bad according to whether these arrangements are pleasing or otherwise. The meaning of the work of art is of no significance; those who are interested in such merely human matters are called Philistines.

This point of view belongs only to the last few centuries in Europe, and to the decadence of classical civilization in the Mediterranean. It has not been endorsed by humanity at large, and may be quite a false view. According to another and quite different assumption, which prevailed throughout the Middle Ages in Europe and is in fact proper to the Christian as well as the Hindu philosophy of life, art is primarily an intellectual act; it is the conception of form, corresponding to an idea in the mind of the artist. It is not when he observes nature with curiosity, but when the intellect is self-poised, that the forms of art are conceived. The artist is not a special kind of man, but every man is a special kind of artist or else is something less than a man. The engineer and the cook, the mathematician and the surgeon are also artists. Everything made by man or done skilfully is a work of art, a thing made by art, artificial.

The things to be made by art in imitation of the imagined forms in the mind of the artist are called true when these imagined forms are really embodied and reproduced in the wood or stone or in the sounds which are the artist's material. He has always in view to make some definite thing, not merely something beautiful, no matter what; what he loves is the particular thing he is making; he knows that anything well and truly made will be beautiful. Just what is to be made is a matter for the patron to decide; the artist himself if he is building his own house, or another person who needs a house, or in the broadest sense the patron, is the artist's whole human environment, for example when he is building a temple or laying out a city. In unanimous societies, as in India, there is general agreement as to what is most needed; the artist's work is therefore generally understood; where everyone makes daily use of works of art there is little occasion for museums, books or lectures on the appreciation of art.

The thing to be made, then, is always something humanly useful. No rational being works for indefinite ends. If the artist makes a table, it is to put things on; if he makes an image, it is as a support for contemplation. There is no division of fine or useless from decorative and useful arts; the table is made to give intellectual pleasure as well as to support a weight, the image gives sensual, or as some prefer to call it, aesthetic pleasure at the same time that it provides a support for contemplation.

There is no caste division of the artist from the workman such as we are inured to in industrial societies where, as Ruskin so well expressed it, "Industry without art is brutality."

In this kind of art there is no demand for novelty, because the fundamental needs of humanity are always and everywhere the same. What is required is originality, or vitality. What we mean by "original" is "coming from its source within", like water from a spring. The artist can only express what is in him, what he is. It makes no difference whether or not the same thing has been expressed a thousand times before. There can be no property in ideas. The individual does not make them, but finds them; let him only see to it that he really takes possession of them, and his work will be original in the same sense that the recurrent seasons, sunrise and sunset are ever new although in name the same. The highest purpose of Christian and Eastern art alike is to reveal that one and the same principle of life that is manifested in all variety. Only modern art, reflecting modern interests, pursues variety for its own sake and ignores the sameness on which it depends.

Finally, the Indian artist, although a person, is not a personality; his personal idiosyncracy is at the most a part of his equipment, and never the occasion of his art. All of the greatest Indian works are anonymous, and all that we know of the lives of Indian artists in any field could be printed in a tract of a dozen pages.

Let us now consider for a short time the history of Indian art. Our knowledge of it begins about 3000 B.C. with what is known as the Indus Valley culture. Extensive cities with well-built houses and an elaborate drainage system have been excavated and studied. The highest degree of artistic ability can be recognized in the engraved seals, sculptured figures in the round, finely wrought jewellery, silver and bronze vessels and painted pottery. From the *Ṛgveda*, the Bible of India, datable in its present form about 1000 B.C., we learn a good deal about the arts of the carpenter, weaver and jeweller.

The more familiar Indian art of the historical period has been preserved abundantly from the third century B.C. onwards.

The greater part of what has survived consists of religious architecture and sculpture, together with some paintings, coins, and engraved seals. The sculptures have been executed in the hardest stone with steel tools. From the sculptures and paintings themselves we can gather a more detailed knowledge of the other arts. The temples are often as large as European cathedrals. Almost peculiar to India has been the practice of carving out such churches in the living rock, the monolithic forms repeating those of the structural buildings. Amongst notable principles developed early in India which have had a marked influence on the development of architecture in the world at large are those of the horse-shoe arch and transverse vault.

An increasing use is made of sculpture. As in other countries, there is a stylistic sequence of primitive, classical, and baroque types. The primitive style of Bhārhut and Sāñcī can hardly be surpassed in significance and may well be preferred for the very reason that it restricts itself to the statement of absolute essentials and is content to point out a direction which the spectator must follow for himself. Nevertheless, in many ways, the Gupta period, from the fourth to the sixth centuries A.D., may be said to represent the zenith of Indian art. By this time the artist is in full and facile command of all his resources. The paintings of Ajaṇṭā, approximately comparable to those of the very early Renaissance in Europe, depict with irresistible enchantment a civilization in which the conflict of spirit and matter has been resolved in an accord such as has hardly been realised anywhere else, unless perhaps in the Far East and in Egypt. Spirituality and sensuality are here inseparably linked and seem to be merely the inner and outer aspects of one and the same expanding life. The art of this age is classical, not merely within the geographical limits of India proper, but for the whole of the Far East, where all the types of Buddhist art are of Indian origin.

There follows a mediaeval period which was essentially an age of devotion, learning and chivalry; the patronage of art and literature moving together as a matter of course.

From the twelfth century onwards, the situation is profoundly modified so far as the North of India is concerned by the impact of Muhammadan invasions of Persian and Central Asian origin. But while the effects of these invasions were to an appalling extent destructive, the Islamic art added something real and valuable to that of India; and finally, though only for a short time, under the Great Mughals in the 16th and 17th centuries, there developed in India a new kind of life which found expression in a magnificent architecture and a great school of painting. Just because of its more humanistic and worldly preoccupations, this art is better known to and better appreciated by Europeans at the present day than is the more profound art of Hindu India. Everyone has heard of the Taj Mahal, a wonder of inlaid marble built by Shāh Jahān to be the tomb of a beloved wife; everyone can easily understand and therefore admire the Mughal paintings that provide us with a faithful portrait gallery of all the great men of Northern India during a period of two centuries. This is a kind of art that really corresponds to that of the late Renaissance, with all its personal, historic and romantic interests.

In the meantime, Hindu culture persisted almost unchanged in the South. In the great temple cities of the South both the reality and the outward aspects of the ancient world have survived until now and the world has no more wonderful spectacle to offer than can be seen here. In the North, Hindu culture survived too in Rajputana and the Punjab Himalayas and here, in direct continuity with ancient tradition, there developed the two schools of Rajput painting that are the last great expressions of the Indian spirit in painting or sculpture. Modern developments in Bengal and Bombay represent attempts either to recover a lost tradition or for the development of an eclectic style, neither wholly Indian nor wholly European. At the present day the Indian genius is finding expression rather in the field of conduct than in art.

European influence on Indian art has been almost purely destructive: in the first place, by undermining the bases of patronage, removing by default the traditional responsibilities of wealth to learning. Secondly, the impact of industrialism, similarly undermining the status of the responsible craftsman, has left the consumer at the mercy of the profiteer and no better off than he is in Europe. Thirdly, by the introduction of new styles and fashions, imposed by the prestige of power, which the Indian people have not been in a position to resist. A reaction against these influences is taking place at the present day, but can never replace what has been lost; India has been profoundly impoverished, intellectually as well as economically, within the last hundred years.

Even in India, an understanding of the art of India has to be rewon; and for this, just as in Europe where the modern man is as far from understanding the art of the Middle Ages as he is from that of the East, a veritable intellectual rectification is required. What is needed in either case is to place oneself in the position of the artist by whom the unfamiliar work was actually made and in the position of the patron for whom the work was made: to think their thoughts and to see with their eyes. For so long as the work of art appears to us in any way exotic, bizarre, quaint or arbitrary, we cannot pretend to have understood it. It is not to enlarge our collection of bric-a-brac that we ought to study ancient or foreign arts, but to enlarge our own consciousness of being.

As regards India, it has been said that "East is East and West is West and never the twain shall meet." This is a counsel of despair that can only have been born of the most profound disillusion and the deepest conviction of impotence. I say on the contrary that human nature is an unchanging and everlasting principle; and that whoever possesses such a nature—and not merely the outward form and habits of the human animal—is endowed with the power of understanding all that belongs to that nature, without respect to time or place.

SUPPLEMENTARY BIBLIOGRAPHY

The following are important for nearly all periods of Indian art, and are indispensable for some. They are not already quoted in the previous lists.

Avalon, A.: *Principles of Tantra.* London, 1911.

Tantra of the Great Liberation. London, 1913.

Barnett, L.D.: *Hindu Gods and Heroes.* London, 1922.

Basu, B.D., ed.: *Sacred Books of the Hindus.*

Bhagavan Das and Besant, A.: *The Bhagavad-Gītā.* Benares.

Bhandarkar, R.G.: *Vaiṣṇavism, Śaivism and Minor Religious Systems.* Grundriss der Indo-Arischen Philologie und Alterthumskunde, III, 6. Strassburg, 1913.

Bhattacharya, B.C.: *Indian Images.* Calcutta, 1922.

Birdwood, Sir G.: *Industrial Arts of India.* London, 1880.

Burgess, J.: *The Ancient Monuments, Temples and Sculptures of India.* 2 Vols. London, 1897, 1911.

Coomaraśwamy, A.K.: *The Indian Craftsman,* London, 1909. *Arts and Crafts of India and Ceylon.* London, 1913. *Viśvakarma,* London, 1914. *The Mirror of Gesture.* Cambridge, U.S.A., 1917. *Catalogue of the Indian Collections in the Museum of Fine Arts,* Boston, 1923.

Deussen, P.: *The Philosophy of the Upanishads.* Edinburgh, 1908.

Fergusson, J.: *History of Indian and Eastern Architecture,* revised edition. London, 1910.

Fonseka, L. de: *On the Truth of Decorative Art.* London, 1912.

Getty, A.: *The Gods of Northern Buddhism.* Oxford, 1914.

Grünwedel, A.: *Buddhist Art in India.* London, 1901.

Havell, E.B.: *Indian Sculpture and Painting.* London, 1908. *Ideals of Indian Art.* London, 1911. *Indian Architecture.* London, 1913. *Ancient and Mediaeval Architecture of India.* London, 1915. *History of Aryan Rule in India.* London, 1918. *Handbook of Indian Art.* London, 1920.

Keith, A.B.: *Mythology of all Races,* Vol. 6, Iranian and Indian. Boston, 1916.

Kern, H.: *Manual of Indian Buddhism,* Grundriss der Indo-Arischen Philologie und Alterthumskunde. Strassburg, 1896.

Mukherji, T.N.: *Art Manufactures of India.* Calcutta, 1888.

Müller, Max, ed.: *Sacred Books of the East.*

Nahar, P.C., and Ghosh, K.: *Epitome of Jainism.* Calcutta, 1917.

Okakura Kakuzo: *Ideals of the East.* New York, 1904.

Rao, T.A.G. : *Elements of Hindu Iconography.* Madras, 1914-1916.
Rapson, E.J., ed. : *The Cambridge History of India.* Cambridge, 1922.
Ray, P.C. : *The Mahabharata* (translation). New Edition. Calcutta, 1922.
Rhys-Davids, T.W. : *Dialogues of the Buddha,* 3 Vols. London, 1899-1920.
Sastri, H.K. : *South Indian Gods and Goddesses.* Madras, 1916.
Smith, V.A. : *History of Fine Art in India and Ceylon.* Oxford, 1911.
Watt, Sir G. : *Indian Art at Delhi.* London, 1904.

NOTES ON ILLUSTRATIONS

Fig. 1. Limestone statue of a man, Mohenjo-Daro. *ca.* 2000-3000 B.C. Indo-Sumerian. Third millennium B.C.

Figs. 2-6. Seals or plaques with various devices and pictographic script, from Mohenjo-Daro. Third millennium B.C.: 2. with humped Indian bull; 3. with bull; 4. with bull or 'unicorn'; 5. with elephant; 6. sacred tree (*pippala, Ficus religiosa*), with animal heads with long necks attached to the stem.

Fig. 7. Plaque, representing a nude goddess, probably the Earth. From the Vedic burial mound at Lauṛiyā-Nandangaṛh. Seventh or eighth century B.C. Gold.

Fig. 8. Four deer with one head, Ajaṇṭā, Cave I, capital relief *in situ*. Early seventh century A.D.. but an ancient motif.

Fig. 9. Winged goddess, standing on a lotus, from Basāṛh. Moulded terra-cotta. Maurya or older.

Fig. 10. Yakṣa, from Pārkham, now C 1 in the Mathurā Museum. Polished sandstone, 8′ 8″. Maurya or older.

Fig. 11. Yakṣī, from Besnagar, now in the Indian Museum, Calcutta. Sandstone, 6′ 7″. Maurya or older.

Fig. 12. Aśokan pillar. Column set up at Lauṛiyā-Nandangaṛh, Nepal. Sandstone, 32′ 9-1/2″ (base 35-1/2″ diameter, top 22-1/2″). Maurya.

Fig. 13. Sāñcī, Stūpa No. I. East gate and part of railing. Third to first century B.C. Foundations, Maurya; railing and stūpa enlargement, Śuṅga; gates, early Andhra.

Fig. 14. Indra: Relief *in situ*, Bhājā, *vihāra*, west end of verandah, right of cell door. Early Śuṅga or Late Maurya.

Fig. 15. Kuvera Yakṣa. Bhārhut, Northern corner jamb. Sandstone. Height 5′. Middle second century. B.C. Indian Museum, Calcutta.

Fig. 16. Paraśurāmeśvara *liṅgam*, with two-armed representation of Śiva. In *pūja* at Guḍimallam. Polished stone, 5′. First century B.C.

Fig. 17. "Bodhisattva," (Buddha), Mathura. Śākya Muni, the Buddha with shaven head, spiral *uṣṇīṣa*, (inscription). Scalloped halo, Bodhi tree, raining flowers. Buddha seated on a lion throne; two attendants with *caurīs*. Inscription in Brāhmī characters, not dated. Right hand in *abhaya mudrā*, left hand on knee, not clenched. From Kaṭrā mound, Mathurā. Mathurā Museum, now A 1. Early second century. Red sandstone, 2′ 3-1/4″.

Fig. 18. Buddha, Mathurā Museum (Now No. A-21). The arms are broken, but the attitude is that of imparting protection. Two lions symbolize the *siṁhāsana*. Between the lions there is a devotional scene. Cf. illustration given by Sir John H. Marshall, "Notes on Archaeological Exploration in India," *JRAS*, 1909, Pl. III b, facing p. 1064: "This statuette was set up near a shrine at Sītalā-Ghāṭī in Mathurā city, where it was being worshipped, and purchased for the Museum." (*Cat. of the Archaeological Museum at Mathurā*, J. Ph. Vogel, Allahabad, 1910, Plate XVI, p. 53.) Size 1′ 5-1/2″.

Fig. 19. Statue of Kaṇiṣka. From the Māt site, Mathurā, now in the Mathurā Museum. Red sandstone, 5′ 4″. Early second century A.D.

Fig. 20. Sūrya, seated in a chariot drawn by four horses; indistinct objects in the hands, perhaps a lotus and a sword. The deity has small shoulder wings, a large semicircular halo, radiating at the edge. From the Saptasamudri well, Mathurā, now D 46 in the Mathurā Museum. Mottled red sandstone, 2′ 9″. 100 A.D. (?)

Fig. 21. Worship of the Buddha-*pādukā*, from the Amarāvatī Stūpa, Amarāvatī. *ca.* 200 A.D. Marble. Madras Museum. India Office photograph. Late Andhra.

Fig. 22. Buddha, Anurādhapura (Ceylon). *ca.* 200 A.D.? Standing figure of Buddha, on the Ruanweli Dāgaba platform (taken before 1906). Dolomite, over life size.

Fig. 23. Two standing Buddhas, Amarāvatī, now in the Madras Museum. Marble, 6′ 4″. End of second or very early third century. Late Āndhra.

Fig. 24. Buddha seated in *jñāna*, the hands in *dhyāna mudrā*. Anurādhapura, Ceylon. 3rd or 4th century A.D. (?) Dolomite, over life size.

Fig. 25. Buddha from Jamālpur (jail) mound, Mathurā, now A 5 in the Mathurā Museum. Fifth century. Red sandstone, 7′ 2″. Gupta.

Fig. 26. Detail of *toraṇa* pillar representing Kṛṣṇa Govardhanadhara; Mt. Govardhana is shown with many peaks, amongst which are seen two cobras, a lion, and a horse-headed fairy; Kṛṣṇa, *gopas* and *gopīs*, and cattle below. Maṇḍor, Jodhpur State. Sandstone. Fifth century (Kṛṣṇa-līlā scene).

Fig. 27. The Varāha Avatār of Viṣṇu raising the earth from the waters at the commencement of a cycle of creation. At Udayagiri, Bhopal State. *ca.* 400 A.D.

Fig. 28. Bodhisattva Avalokiteśvara. Ajaṇṭā: Cave I, back wall, left of antechamber. Gupta and early Mediaeval. *ca.* 600-650 A.D.

Fig. 29. Śiva and Pārvatī. Upper part of the Mt. Kailāsa relief, Kailāsa, Ellora. Eighth century. Pārvatī turns to Śiva in fear, grasps his arm; the maid takes flight: Siva is unmoved, and holds all fast by pressing down his foot.

Fig. 30. Viṣṇu-Anantaśāyin, relief in the Yamapuri or Mahiṣa-maṇḍapam at Mahābalipuram. First half of seventh century.

Fig. 31. Avalokiteśvara (Bodhisattva Padmapāṇi). Ninth and tenth century. Nepal. Now in the Museum of Fine Arts, Boston (No. 17.2315). Copper, gilt and jewelled, 12-3/8″.

Fig. 32. Viṣṇu (Trivikrama), from Sagardighi, Murshidabad District, now o(2)1/21 in the collection of the Bangiya Sahitya Parishad, Calcutta. Brass, 2′ 1-1/2″. Pāla school of Bengal-Bihar-Orissa, Eleventh or twelfth century.

Fig. 33. Māra dharṣaṇā. Buddha tempted by the daughters of Māra. Borobuḍur, Java. Late eighth century.

Fig. 34. Gallery relief. Part of the procession of an army, southern gallery, left side. (Army of King Sūryavarman II, 1112-1152). Angkor Wat, Cambodia. Middle twelfth century.

Fig. 35. Frieze of danseuse. Tejapāla's Jain temple, Mt. Ābu, ceiling. 1230 A.D. Mid Mediaeval.

Fig. 36. Naṭarāja: Śiva, Lord of the Dance; from Velankanni, Negapatam Taluk, Tanjore District. Madras Museum. Copper, height. 84 cm. Late Mediaeval.

Fig. 37. Māṇikka Vāsagar, Śaiva saint and psalmist: right hand in *vitarka mudrā*, left holding a palm-leaf manuscript, inscribed with the formula *Namaśivāya*, 'Hail to Śiva'. Polonnāruva, Śiva Devāle, No. 1, Tenth to thirteenth century. Copper. Height 54·2 cm. Colombo Museum (No. 13.101.286).

Fig. 38. Sundara Mūrti Svāmi, Śaiva saint and psalmist. Polonnāruva, Śiva Devāle, No. 5, Tenth to thirteenth century. Copper. Height 52·7 cm. Colombo Museum (No. 13.99.285). Late Mediaeval.

Fig. 39. Page of a manuscript of the *Kalpasūtra* (Lives of the Jinas), f. 49 with text, and a representation of the *Dīksa* (tonsure) of the Māhavīra. The Jina is seated beneath the *aśoka* tree, in a rocky landscape, plucking out his hair; he is attended by Indra who receives the discarded secular robes and provides those of a monk. Legend: *Mahāvīra loñca*. Thick paper. Western India (Patan in Gujarat?). Fifteenth century. Leaf, 28 x .025 m. Ross-Coomaraswamy Collection. [17.2276]. Museum of Fine Arts, Boston, Massachusetts, U.S.A.

Fig. 40. Sadh Malāra Rāgiṇī, Rājasthānī. Late sixteenth century. Metropolitan Museum of Art, New York. (superscribed *Śrī Rāga* 3. A *yogi* with a *viṇā* seated on the roof of a house, feeding a peacock; clouds, rain, lightning. Belongs to *Rāgamālā* series 2; reverse with a *dohā*. Paper, 5′3/4″ × 7′-7/8″. *ca.* 1600. Pure Rajput (Rājasthānī) style.

Fig. 41. Madhu-mādhavī Rāgiṇī (a musical mode). Princess on a palace terrace, feeding a peacock, attended by four maids, two with dishes, two with musical instruments. The peacocks are excited by the prospect of rain; the lady hears the 'melodious rumbling of the thunder' and longs for her absent lord. Day scene with a stormy sky. Paper. Rajput, Rājasthānī. Sixteenth century. Dimensions, .168 × .250 m. Ross Collection. From a series of pictures illustrating a Hindi *Rāgamālā*, of which the Boston Museum has several examples.

LITERAL TRANSLATION OF THE TEXT:

Madhu-mādhavī is a woman of richest beauty, she wears a green garment over all her body,
Many kinds of jewels adorn her limbs, a myriad sages pale and faint to see her.
Coming from the palace, she stands in the garden: heavy black clouds are joyfully assembled,
The sweet melodious rumbling of thunder is heard, and flashes of lightning light up the sky.
Birds are sporting, with melodious cries of joy, and the princess beholding (all this grandure) stands there delighted.
For the meeting with her darling, her body blossoms like a flower, she stands entranced,
Dreaming of her lord's embrace, there is bliss in her heart.

TEXT OF THE HINDI INSCRIPTION:

Rāganī Madhu-mādhavī: copaī:

Madhu-mādhavī rūpa nīdhīnā nāri,
harita barana pahairai tana sārī;
Bhāvai bheda bhuṣaṇa aṁga nīke,
dekhi koṭi muni saji hoī phīke;
Nikasī mahala bārī mahi ṭhāḍhī,
nīla jalada umagī ghaṭā gāṛhī;
Madhura madhura dhuṇī garajata āvai,
dāmiṇī camakī raba jhalāvai;
Kuralahī[1] khaga' ānaṁda survāṇi,
dekhi surījhī rahī tihī rāṇī.

Dohā:

Pīya mīlāpa ko phula tana, ṭhāḍhī karata vīnoda,
Nṛpahiṁ ḍola kai manabasī, tāthai mana mahī moda.

1 *kuralahī* = *krīdahīṁ*, 'are sporting,' as in the *Padumāvatī* of Muḥammad Jaisī, stanza 33 (ed. Grierson and Dvivedi, Calcutta, 1911).

Fig. 42. The Siege of Laṇkā: Rāma, Lakṣmaṇa, Vibhīṣaṇa, Hanumān, etc., with an army of bears and monkeys encamped before the city walls, two *rākṣasa* spies (Śuka and Sāraṇa), detected by Vibhīṣaṇa, held prisoner. Painting in gold and colours. Pahāṛī, Jamū. Early seventeenth century. Dimensions, .820 × .585 m. Ross-Coomaraswamy Collection.

Reverse with a lengthy extract in Nāgarī characters from the *Rāmāyaṇa* of Vālmīkī. The extract concludes with the rubricated passage:—

Ityārtha Rāmāyaṇe Maharṣi-Vālmīki-viracite Śrī-Rāma-carite caturviṁśati sāhasrām sāṁhitāyām Laṅkākāṇḍe Vibhīṣaṇena Śuka-Sāraṇa-grahaṇam Śuka-Sāraṇau prati Śrī-Rāma-Candra-saroṣa-vākyam:

"Thus the tale of the multifarious *Rāmāyaṇa* of Vālmīki, of twenty-four thousand verses, the Laṅkā-section, the capture of Śuka and Sāraṇa by Vibhīṣaṇa, and the stern speech made by Śrī Rāma Candra to Śuka and Sāraṇa."

A series unique in size (33 × 34 inches) and historical importance, strong in colour and bold but not refined in draughtsmanship, and recalling the mural art from which it undoubtedly derives. The series may originally have consisted of a hundred or more sheets; two paintings and several drawings from the same series are in the Metropolitan Museum of Art, New York. Several examples are endorsed with lengthy extracts from the *Rāmāyaṇa*, written in bold Nāgarī characters and rubricated, but in the drawings the names of personages represented are indicated in several instances in Ṭākṛī script. The paintings have red margins, and as is often the case with Jamū pictures, portions of the picture intrude upon the margin. Above the high horizon there is always a narrow strip of cloudy sky. "...the paintings all belonged to Rajah Raghunath Singh, a former ruler of Guler, an important principality in the Kangra State," (Ajit Ghose, *Roopalekha*, II, p. 5, April, 1929). Six paintings and a number of drawings are in the Boston Museum; two paintings and several drawings are in the Metropolitan Museum of Art, New York, two paintings and several drawings are in the Cleveland Museum of Art, Cleveland, Ohio. [17.2746] Museum of Fine Arts, Boston.

Fig. 43. *Rāmāyaṇa*: Lakṣmaṇa returning from hunting. Lakṣmaṇa shot a deer, which he offers to Rāma with folded hands. Sītā on the right. All are dressed in leaves. Pahāṛī (early Kāṅgṛā), early eighteenth century. Size of the original 7 1/4 × 4 3/4 inches. (Present location unknown.)

Fig. 44. Kṛṣṇa (Veṇugopala) with the flute, standing under a *kadamba* tree, attended by two *gopīs*. Jamunā in the foreground. Soft powdery color. Paper. Rajput, Pahāṛī, Kāṅgṛā. Probably late seventeenth century, early eighteenth. Dimensions, .137 × .181 m. Ross-Coomaraswamy Collection. In mediaeval Vaiṣṇava symbolism, the flute of Kṛṣṇa is the call of Eternity heard by the dwellers in time, represented by the *gopis* or milk-maids of Bṛndāban. Museum of Fine Arts, Boston. 19.132.

INDEX

ILLUSTRATIONS

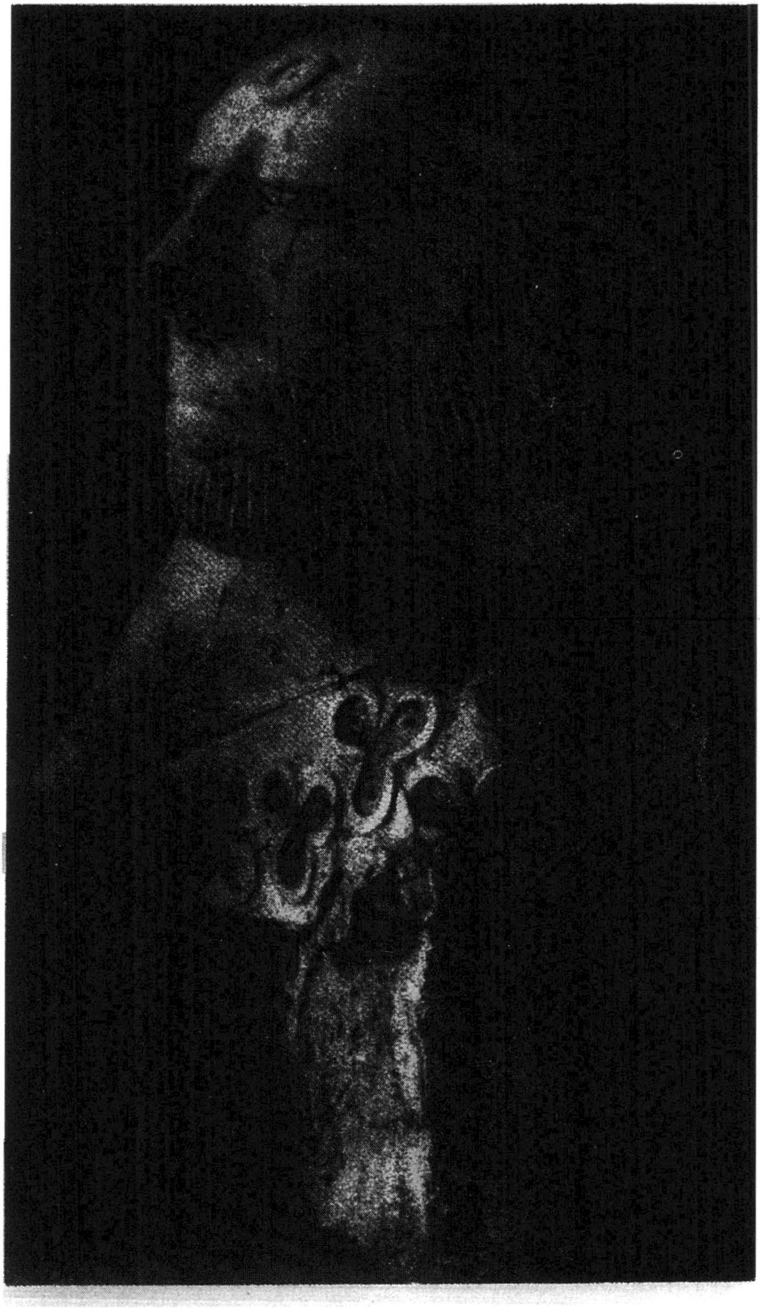

Fig. 1
Statue of a Man
Mohenjo-Daro
ca. **2000-3000** B.C.
Limestone

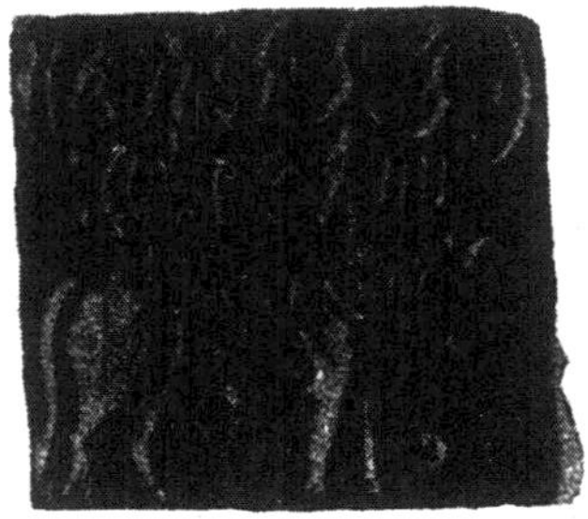

Figs. 2-6. Seals from Mohenjo-Daro. Third Millennium B.C. : 2. *(top left)*. with humped Indian bull; 3. *(top right)*. with bull; 4. *(right)*. with bull or 'unicorn'; 5. *(bottom left)*. with elephant; 6. *(bottom right)*. sacred tree, with animal heads.

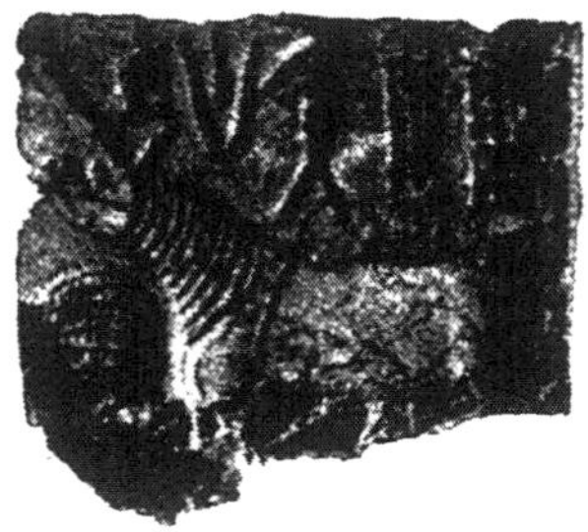

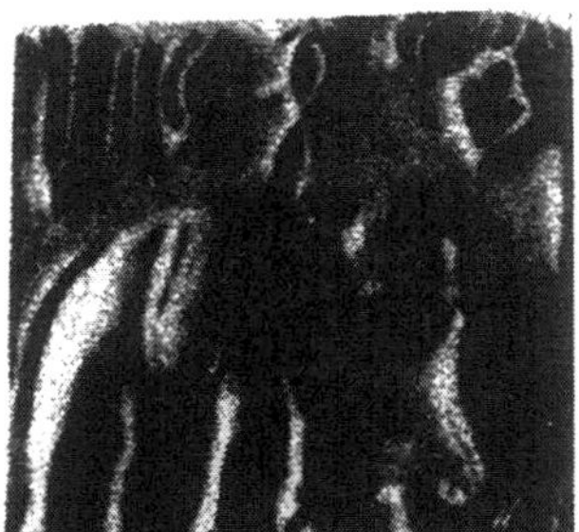

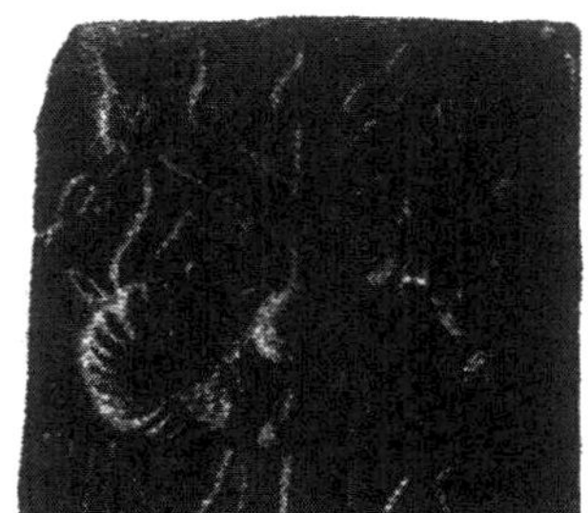

Fig. 7. *(top left)*. **A nude goddess, probably the Earth. From Lauṛiyā-Nandangaṛh, 7th or 8th century** B.C. **Gold. Fig. 8.** *(bottom)*. **Four deer with one head From Ajaṇṭā. Early 7th century** A.D. **Fig. 9.** *(top right)*. **Winged goddess. From Basāṛh. Maurya or older. Moulded terracotta.**

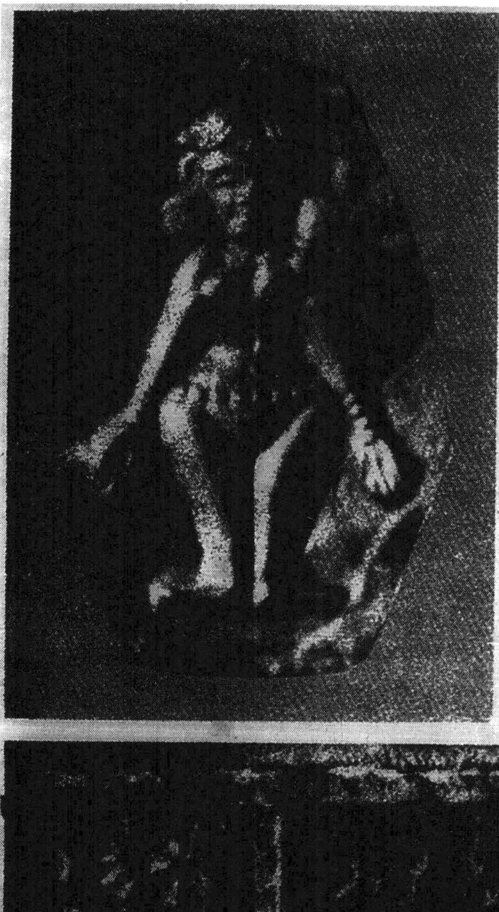

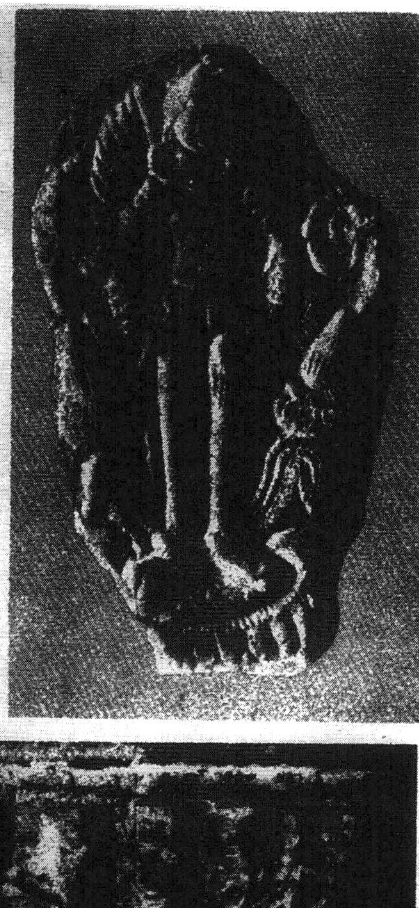

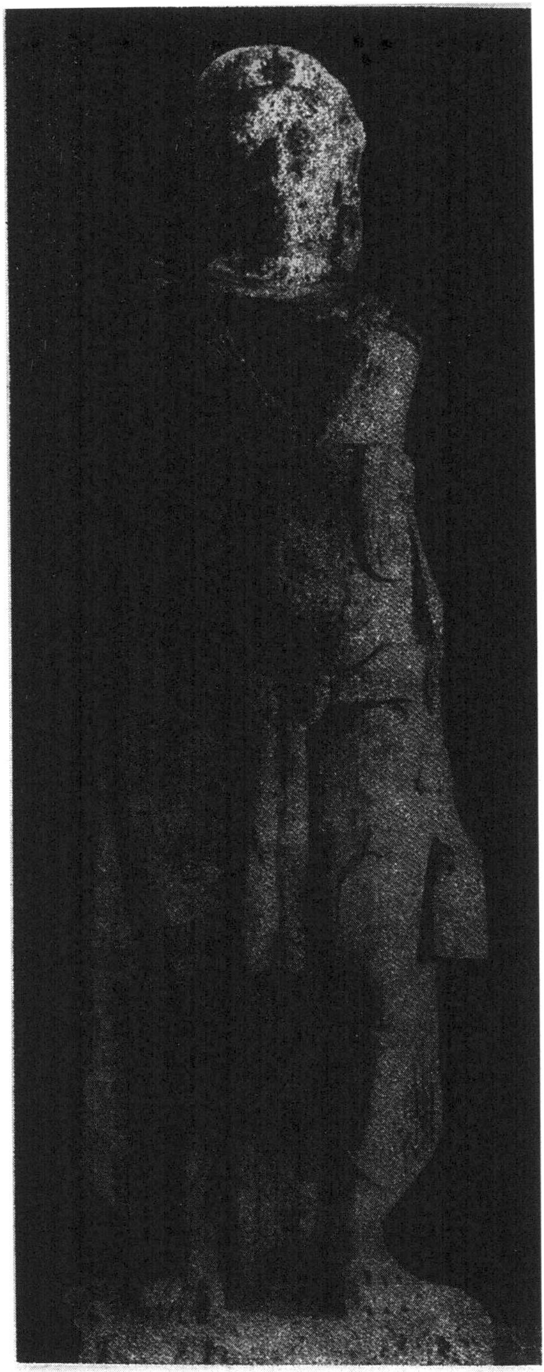

Fig. 10. Yakṣa. From Pārkham
Maurya or older. Polished Sandstone

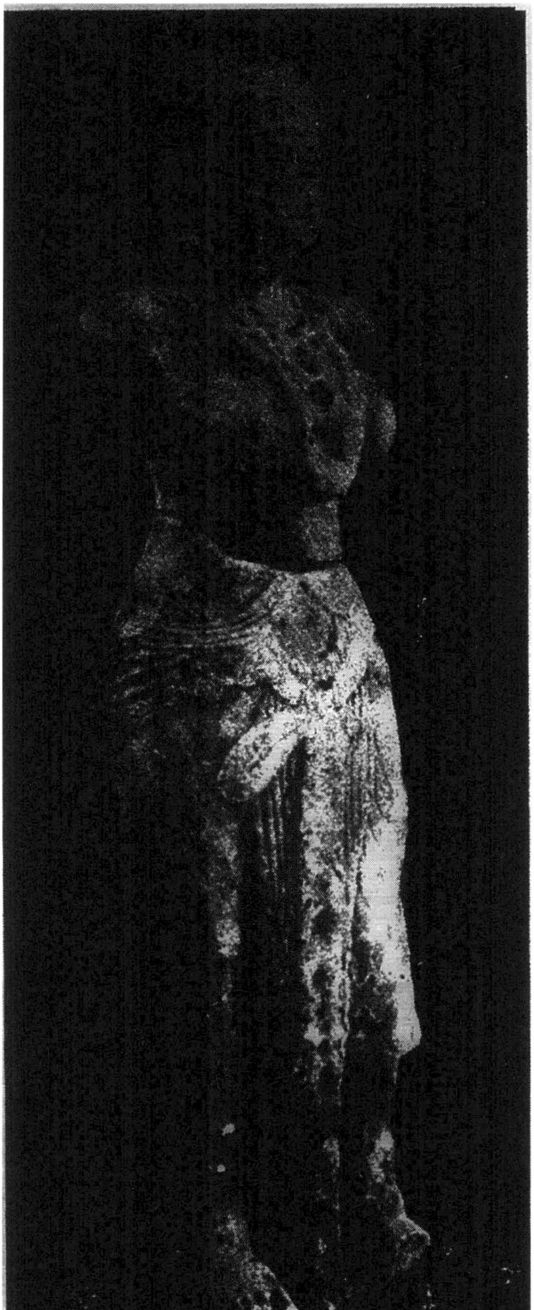

Fig. 11. Yakṣī. From Besnagar Maurya or older. Sandstone

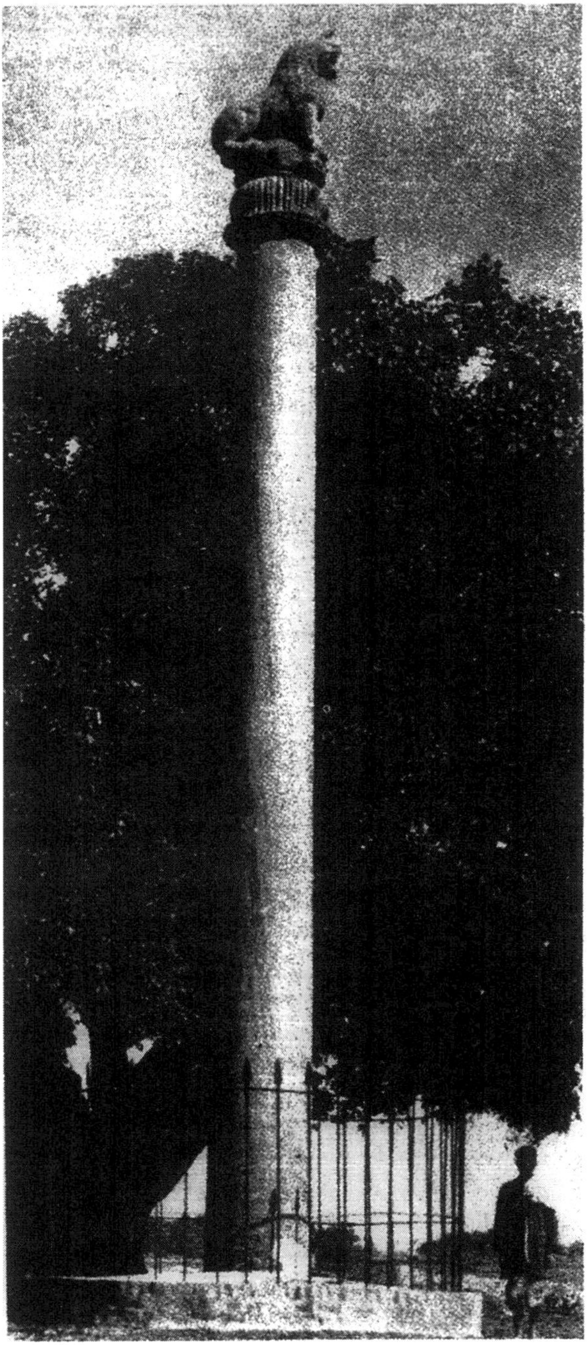

Fig. 12. *(left)*
Lion Column, Aśokan pillar
From Lauṛiyā-Nandangaṛh
3rd century B.C.

Fig. 13. *(right)*
Sāñcī Stūpa
2nd and 1st century B.C. Stone

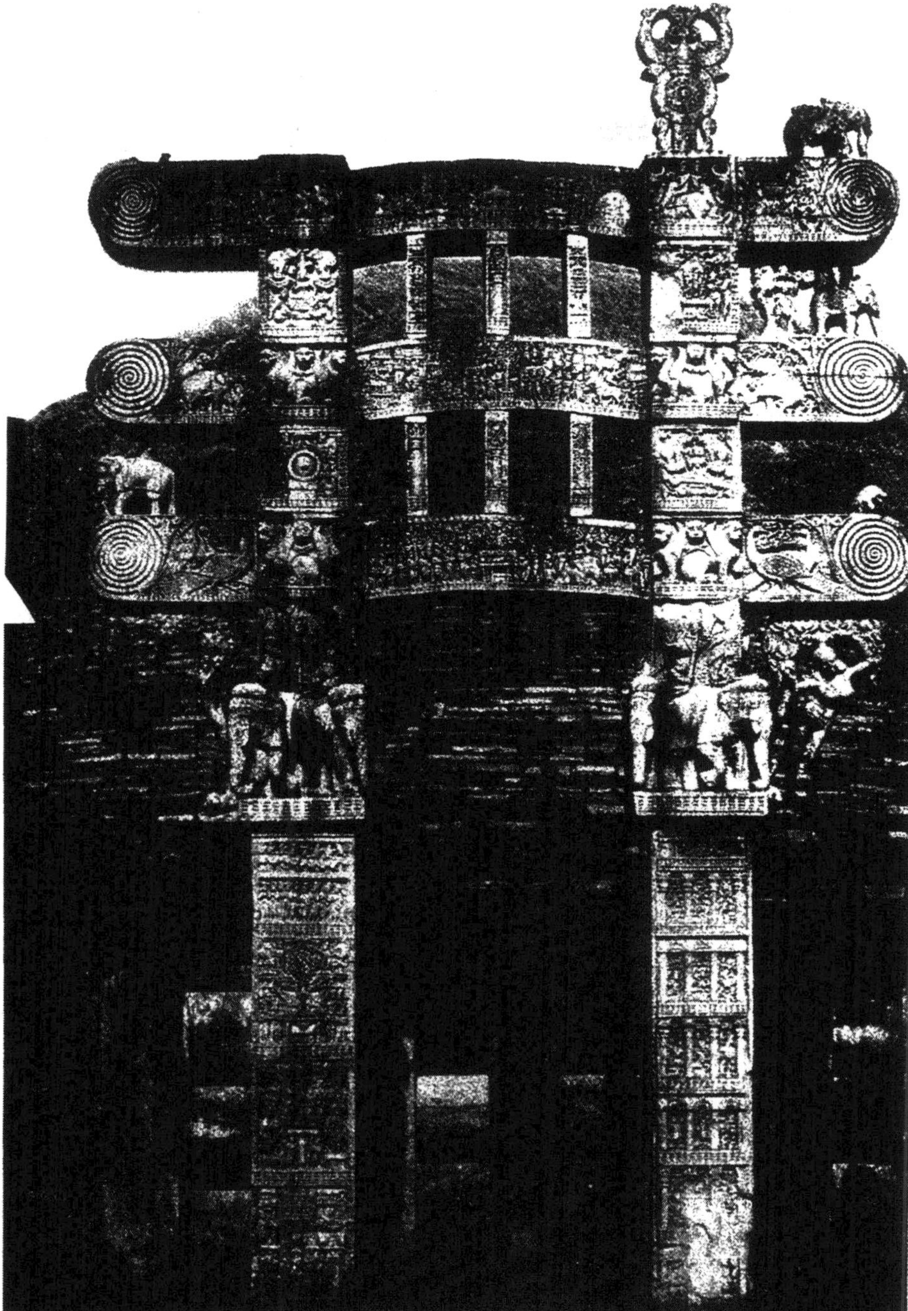

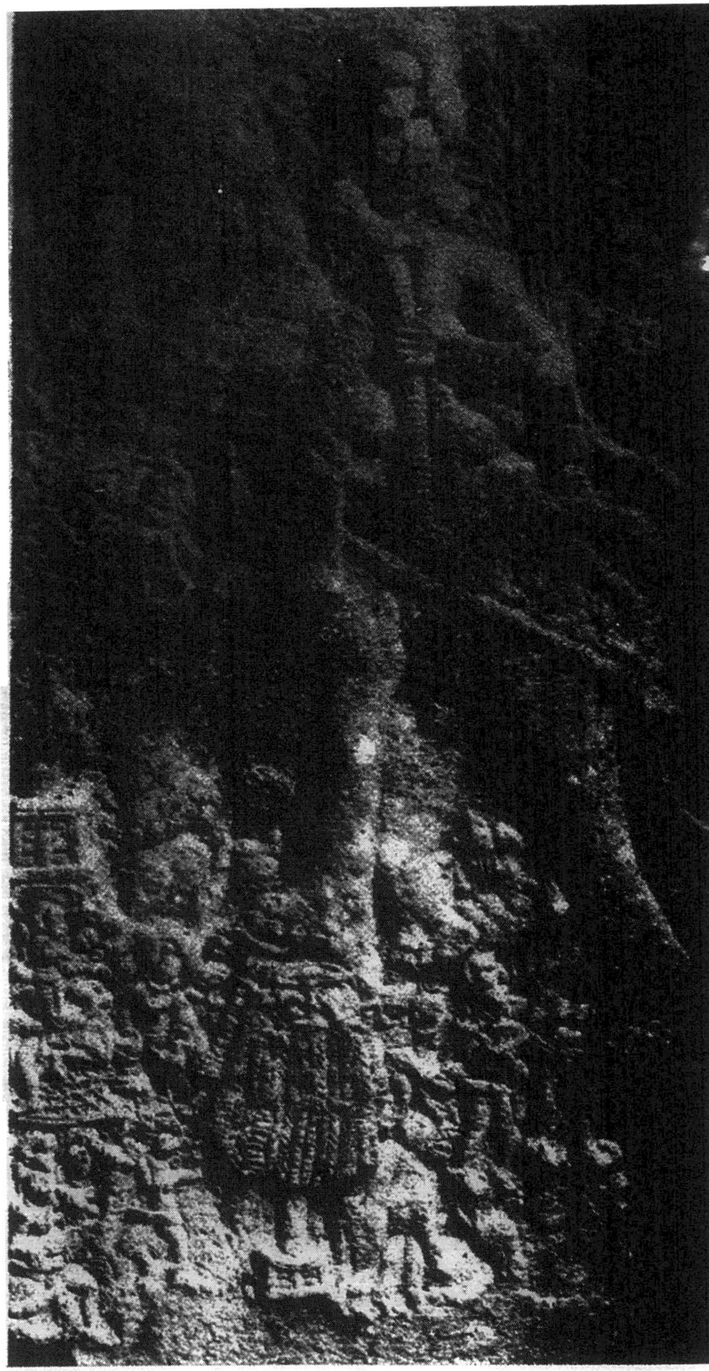

Fig. 14
Indra
From Bhājā vihāra
ca. 2nd century B.C.
Living rock

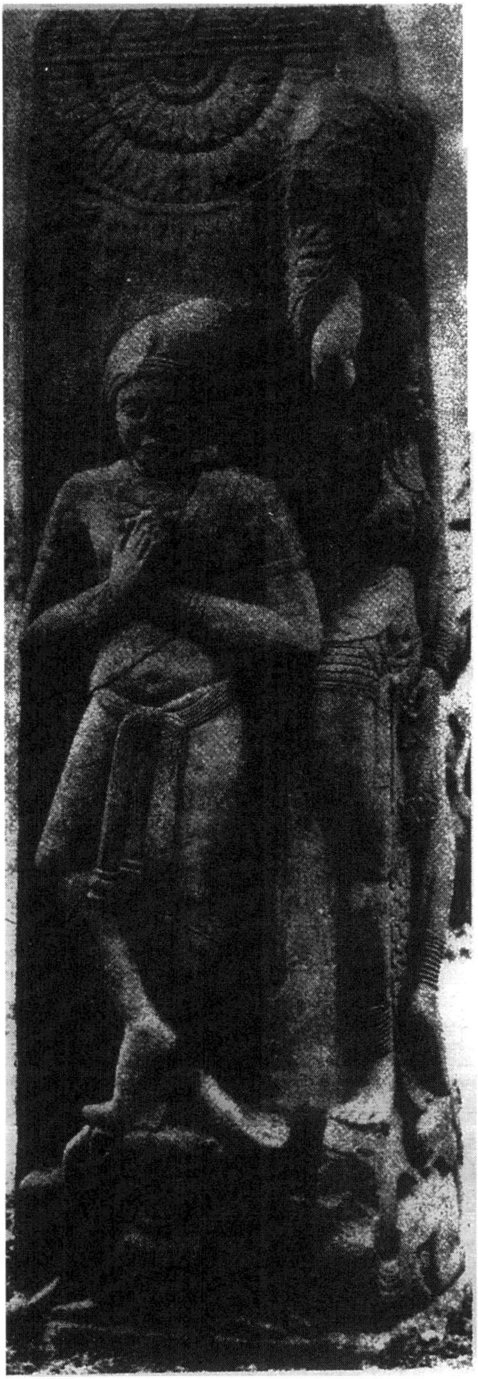

Fig. 15. *(left)*. **Kuvera Yakṣa. From Bhārhut 2nd century B.C. Stone**

Fig. 16. *(bottom)*. **Paraśurāmeśvara liṅgam From Guḍimallam. 1st century B.C. Polished stone**

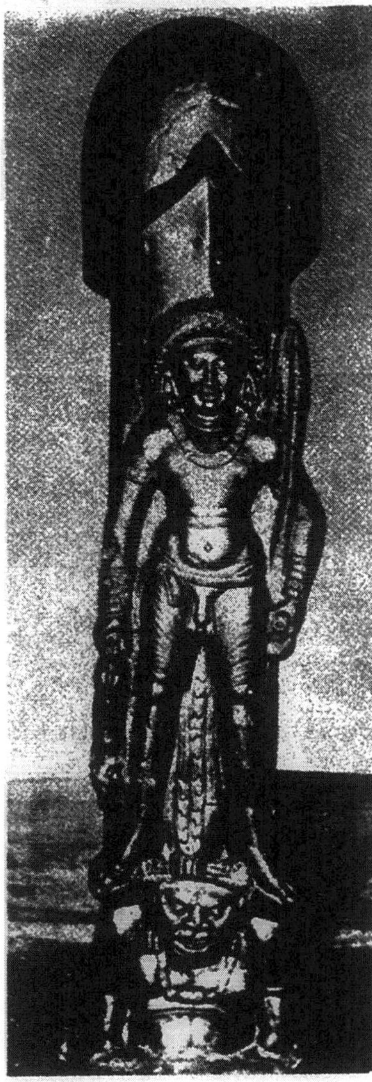

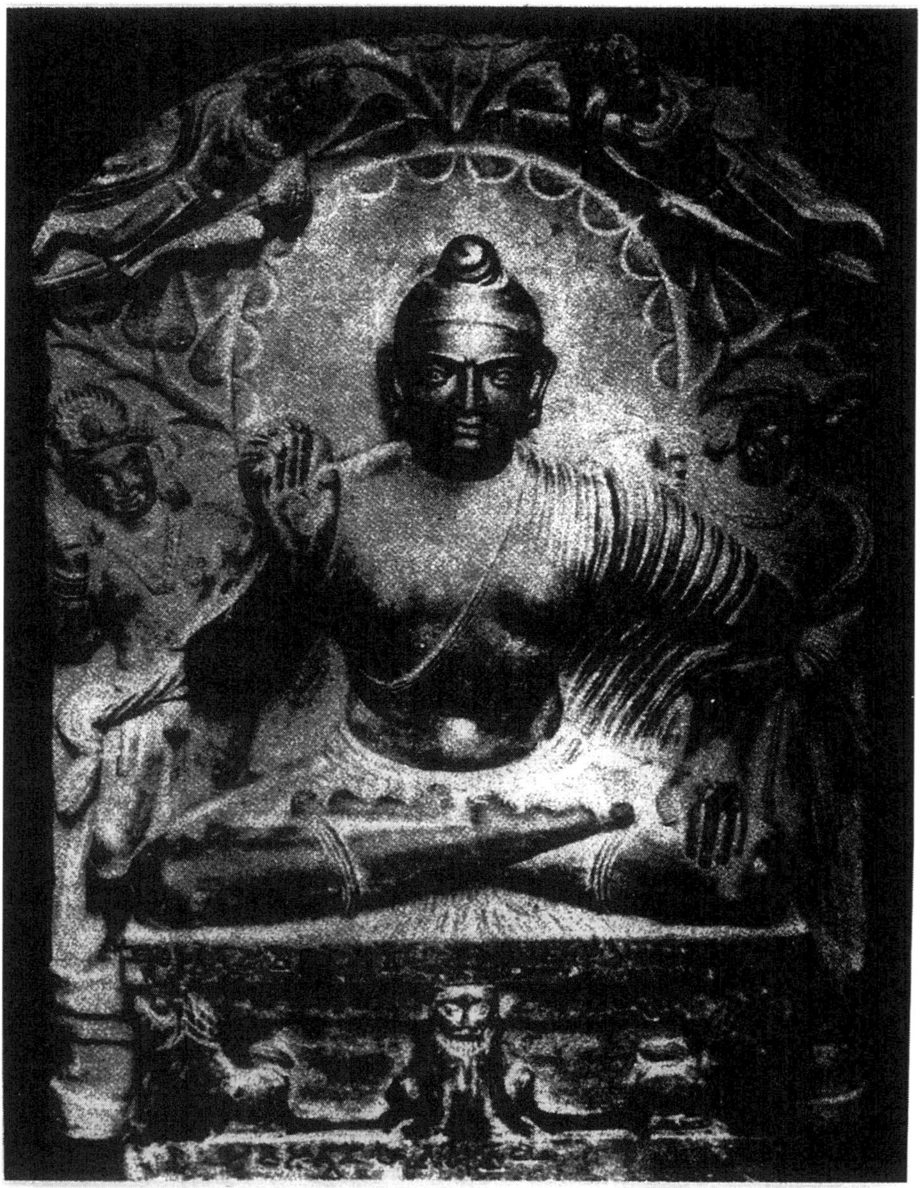

Fig. 17. Bodhisattva, Śākya Muni. From Mathurā, Early 2nd century A.D. Red sandstone.

Fig. 18. Gautama Buddha. 1st century A.D. Stone. Mathurā Museum.

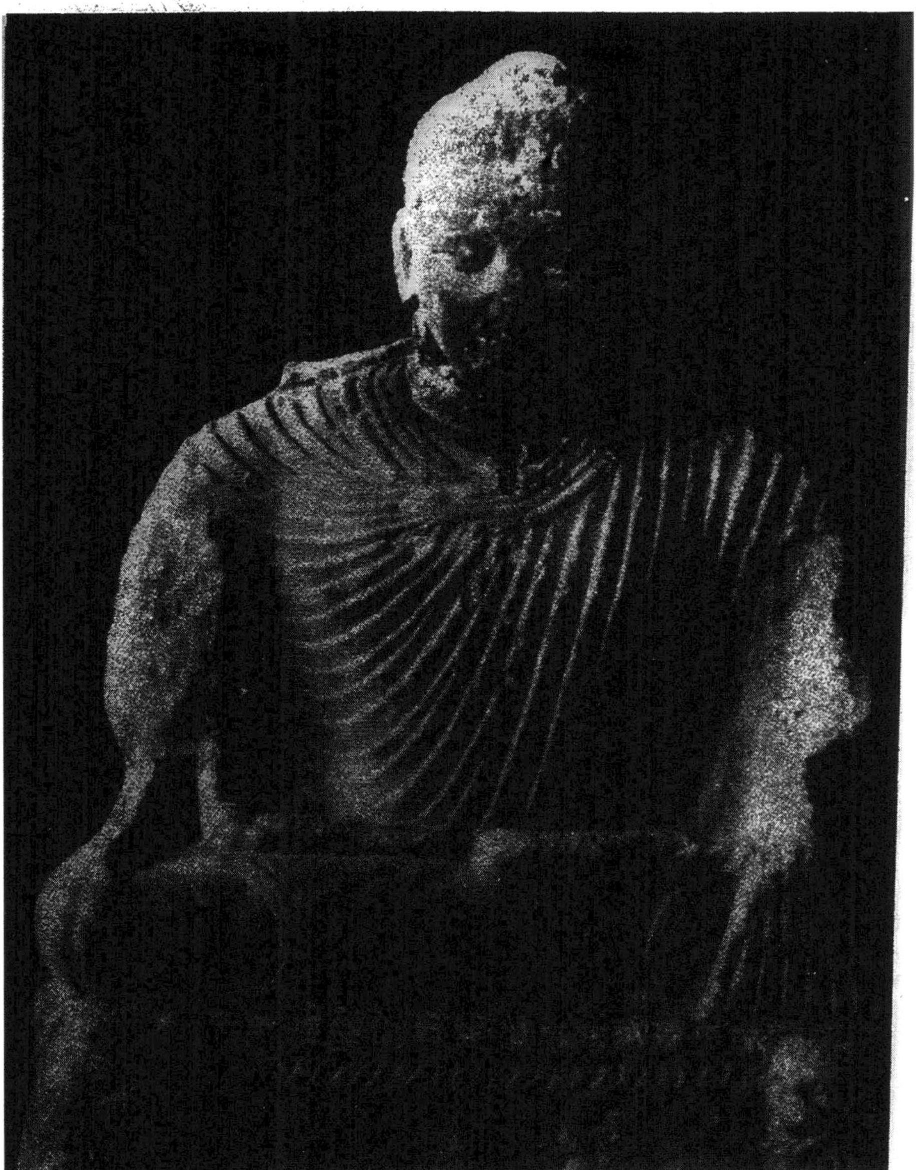

Fig. 19. Kaniṣka. From Mathurā. Early 2nd century A.D. Red sandstone.

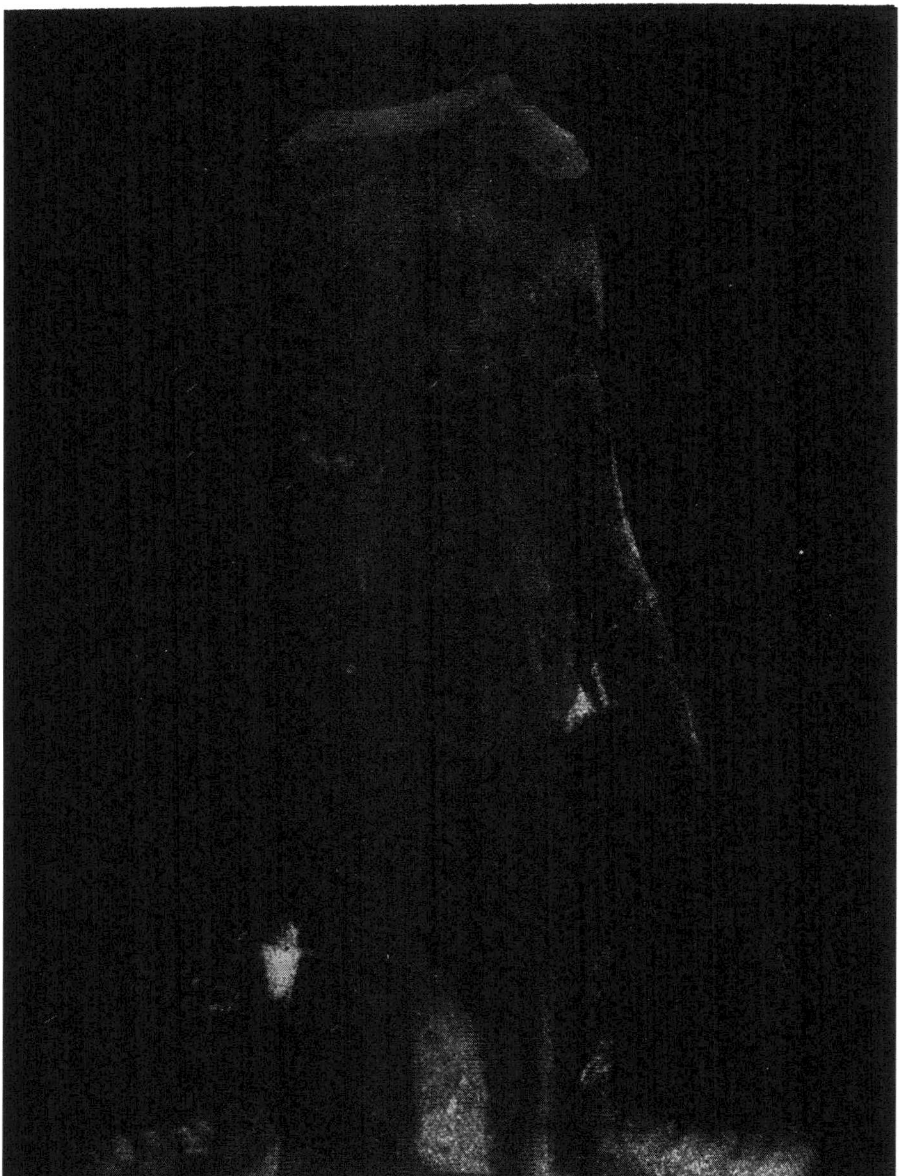

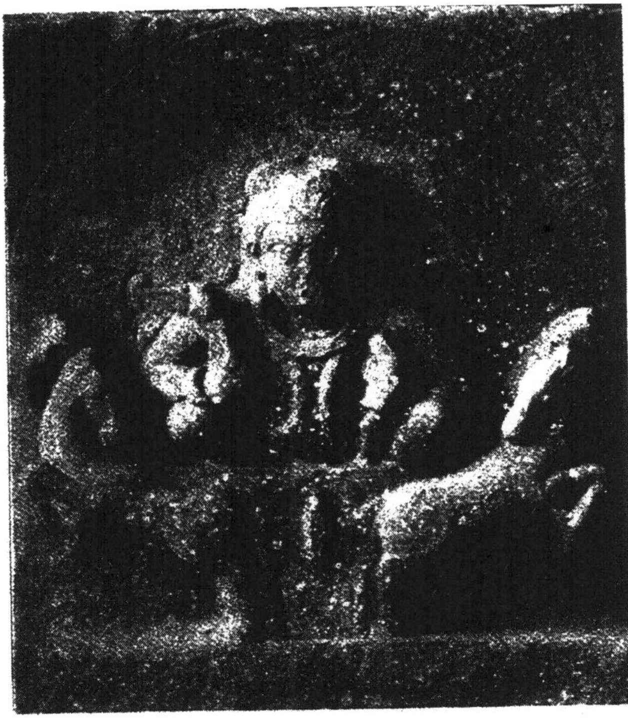

Fig. 20 *(left)*
Sūrya. Frôm Mathurā
ca. 100 A.D. (?).
Mottled red sandstone

Fig. 21. *(bottom)*
Worship of the Buddha-pādukā
From Amarāvatī. *ca.* 200 A.D.

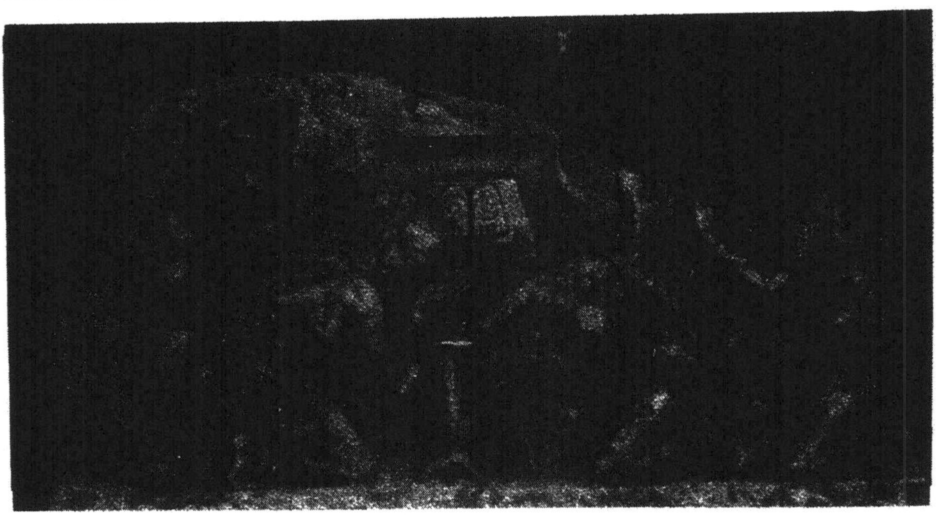

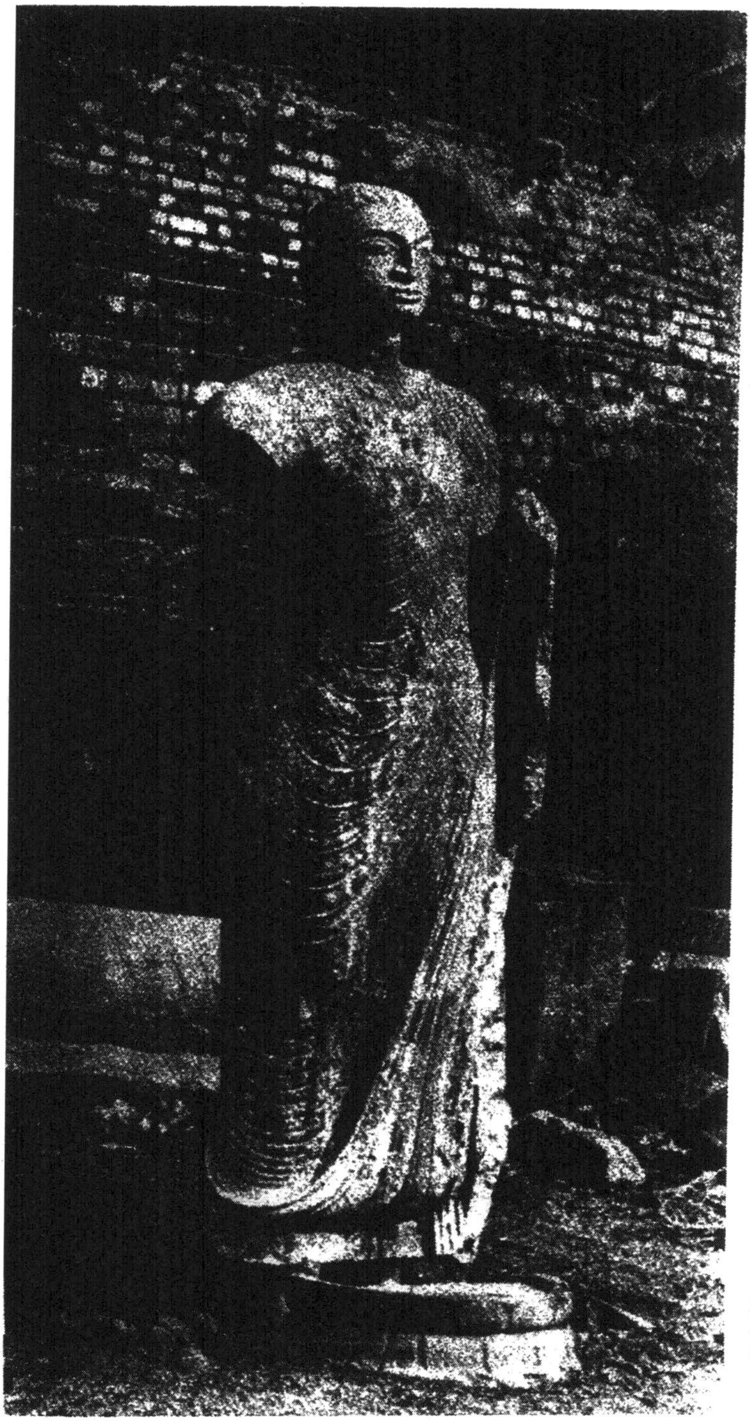

Fig. 22. Buddha. From Anurādhapura, Ceylon *ca.* 200 A.D. **Dolomite**

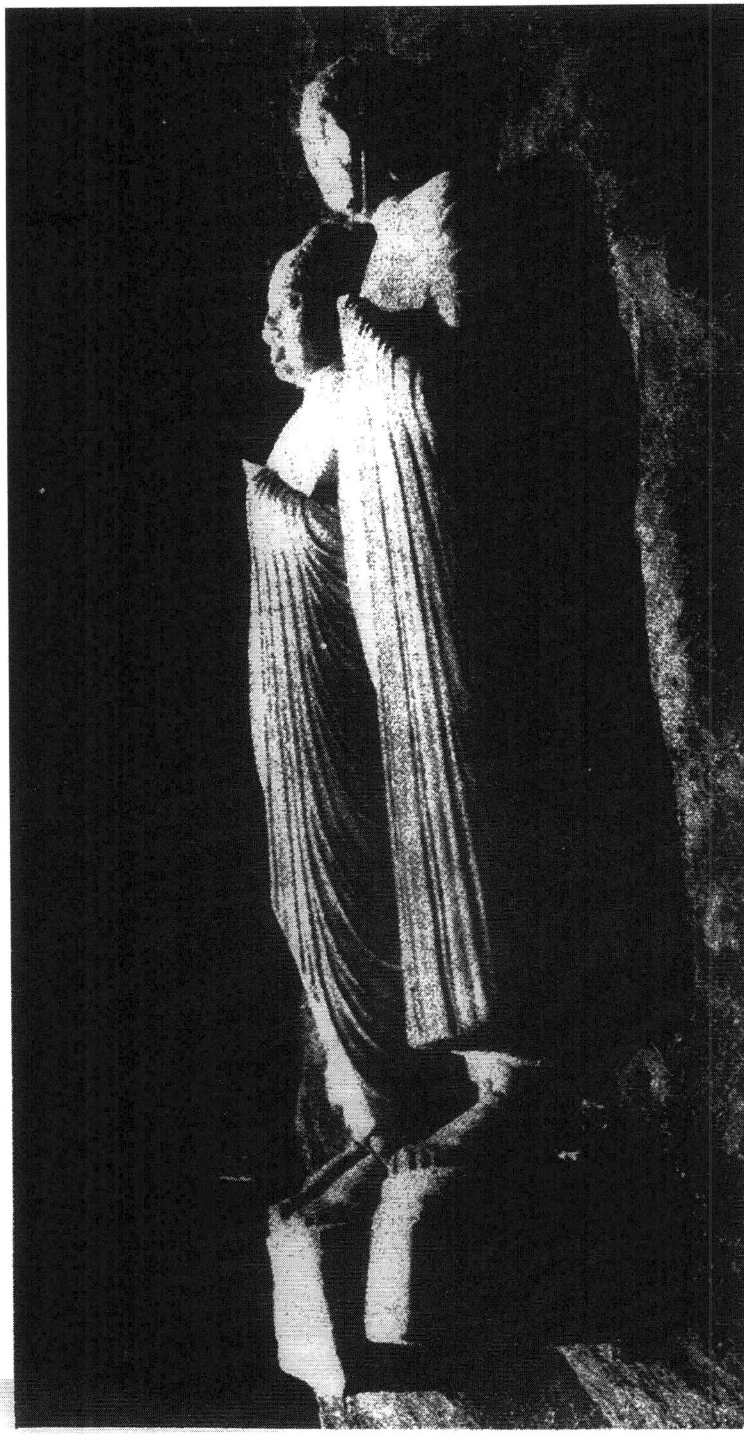

Fig. 23
Two standing Buddhas
From Amarāvatī
2nd century
or very early 3rd
Marble

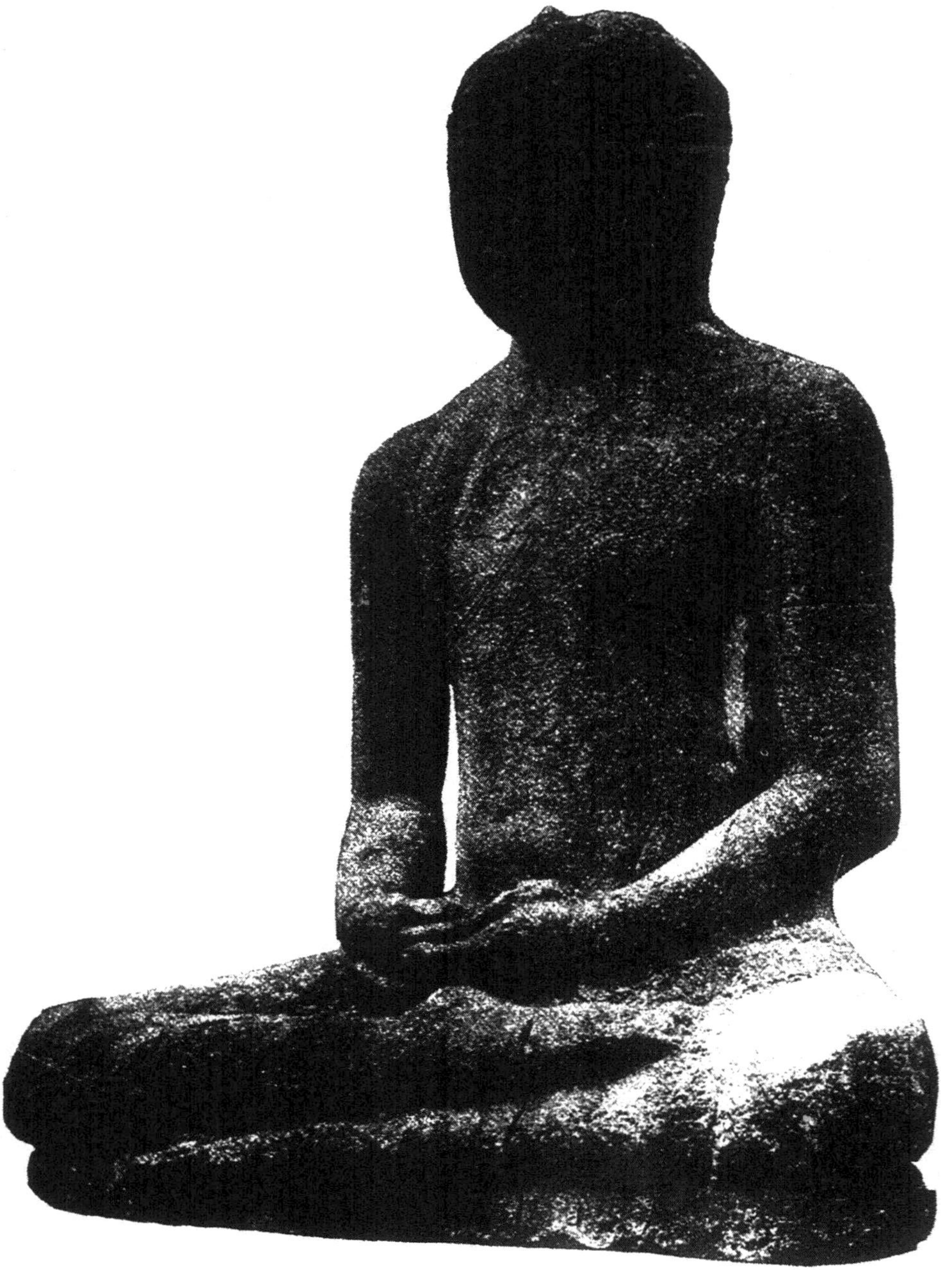

Fig. 24. **Buddha.** From Anurādhapura, Ceylon. 4th century A.D. Dolomite.

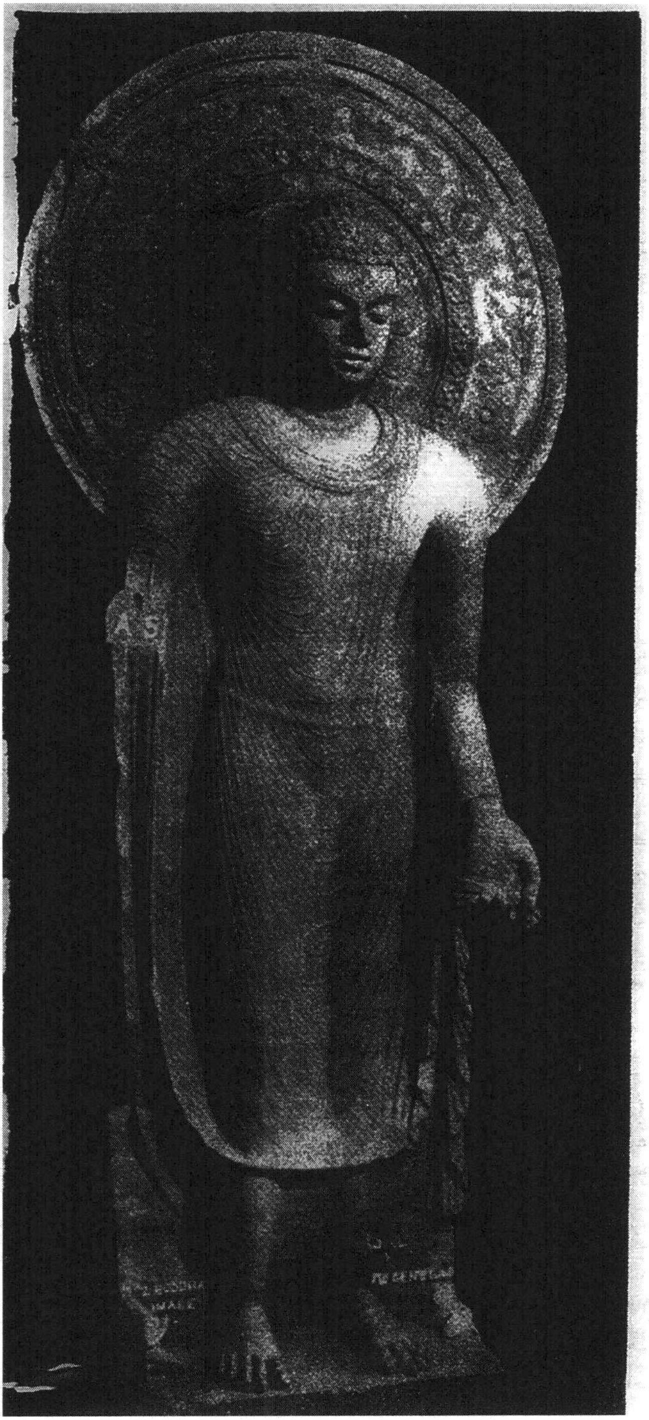

Fig. 25
Buddha. From Mathurā
5th century. Red Sandstone

Fig. 26. *(right)*. Detail of *toraṇa* pillar representing Kṛṣṇa Govardhanadhara. From Maṇḍor. 5th century. Sandstone

Fig. 27. *(bottom)*. Varāha Avatār of Viṣṇu From Udayagiri, Bhopal. *ca.* 400 A.D.

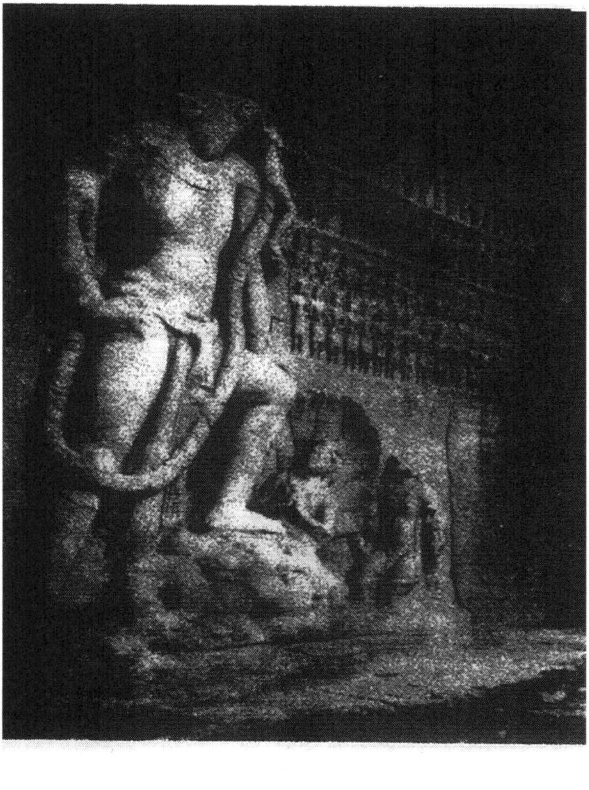

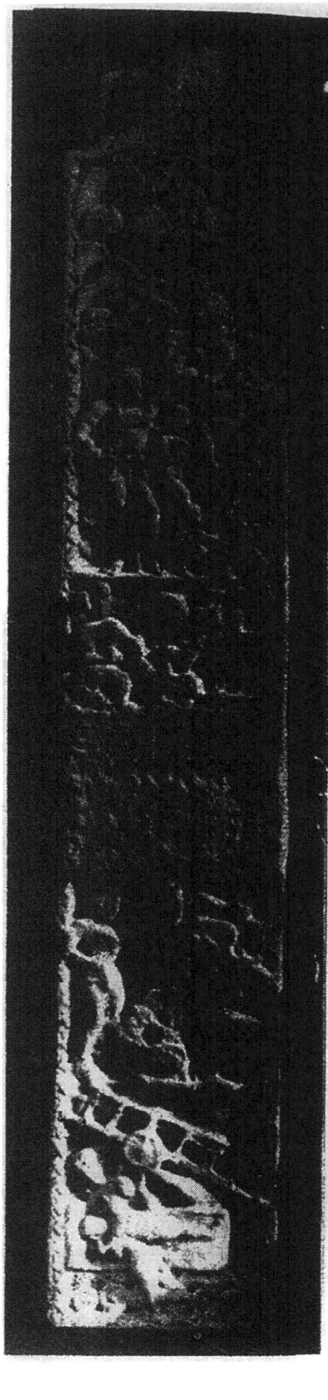

Fig. 28. Bodhisattva Avalokiteśvara. From Ajaṇṭā. *ca.* 600 A.D.

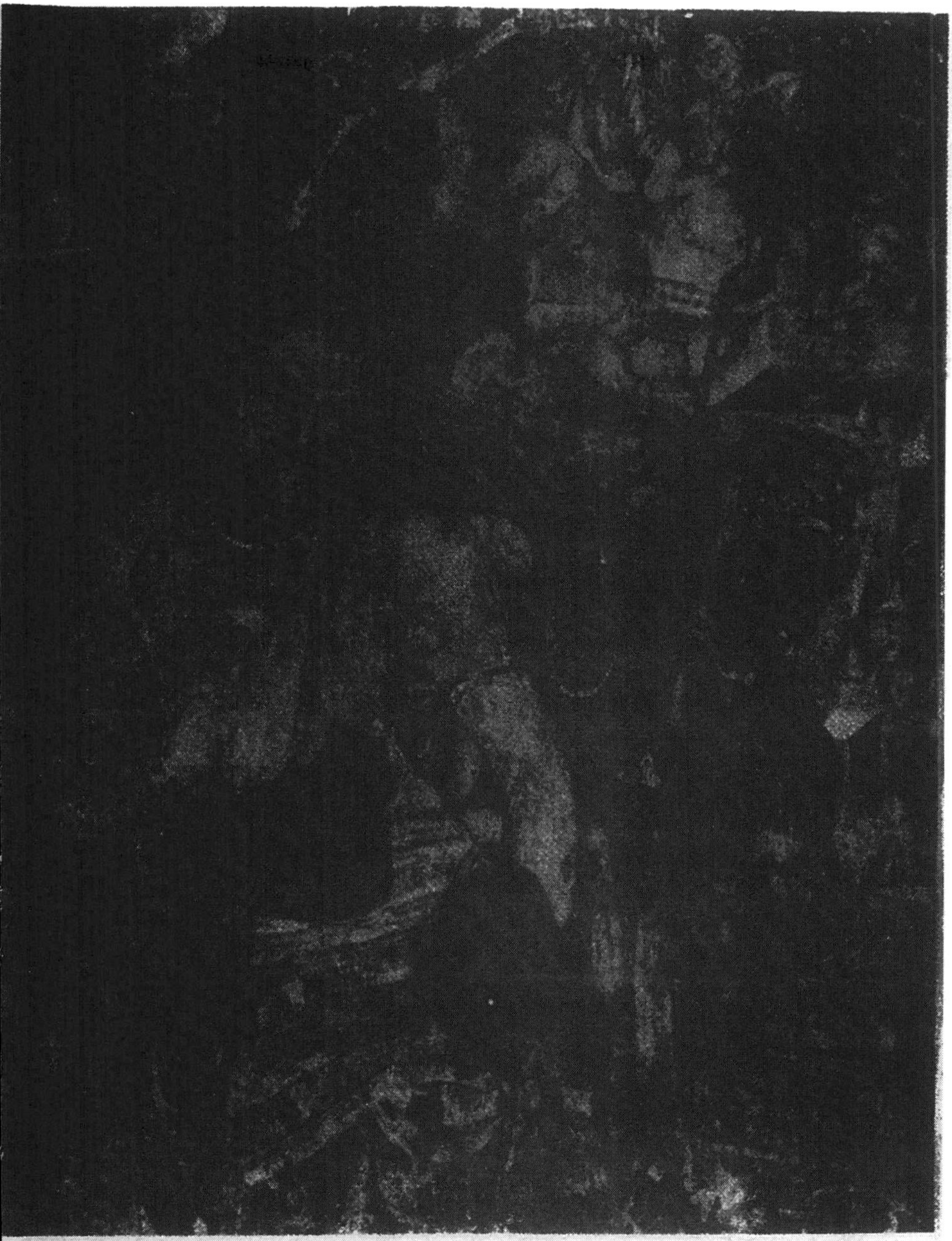

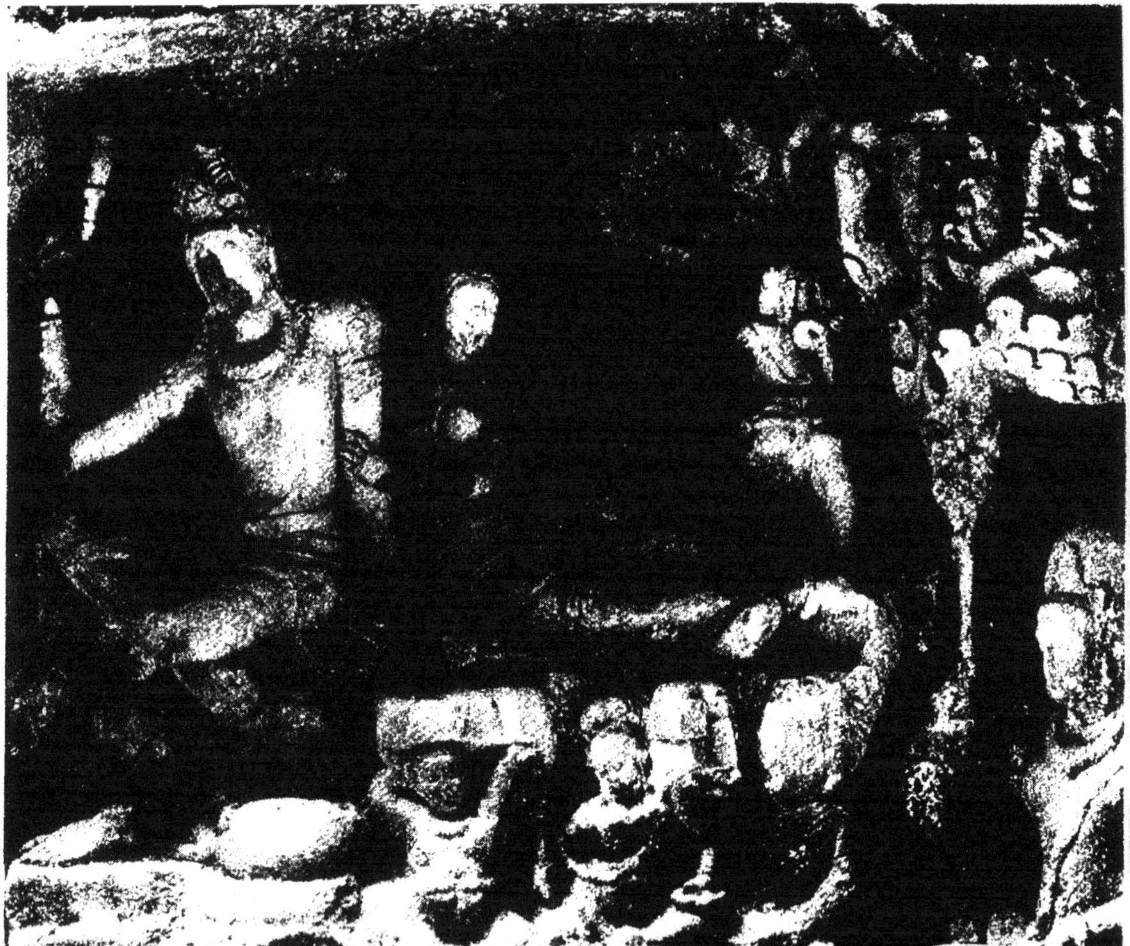

Fig. 29
Śiva and Pārvatī
From Kailāsa, Ellora
8th century

Fig. 30
Viṣṇu-Anantaśāyin
From Mahābalipuram
7th century. Living rock

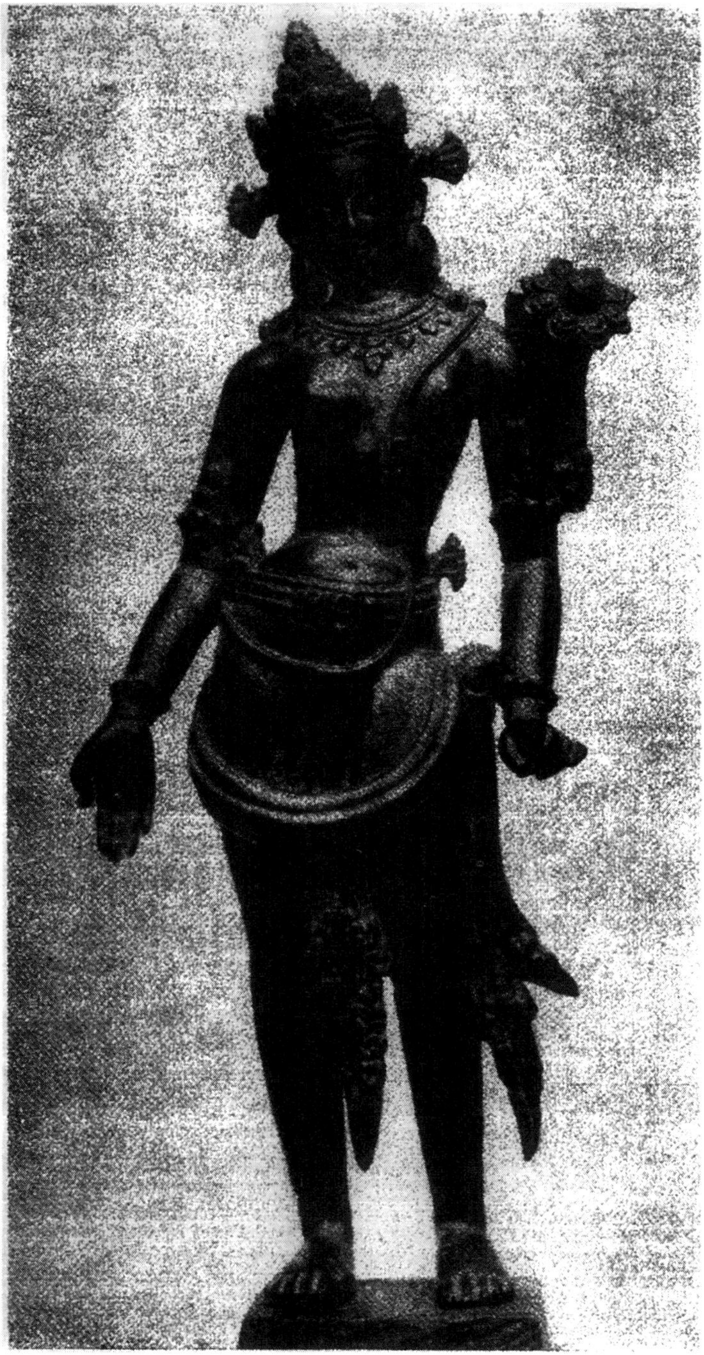

Fig. 31
Bodhisattva
Padmapāṇi
From Nepal
About 10th century
Copper

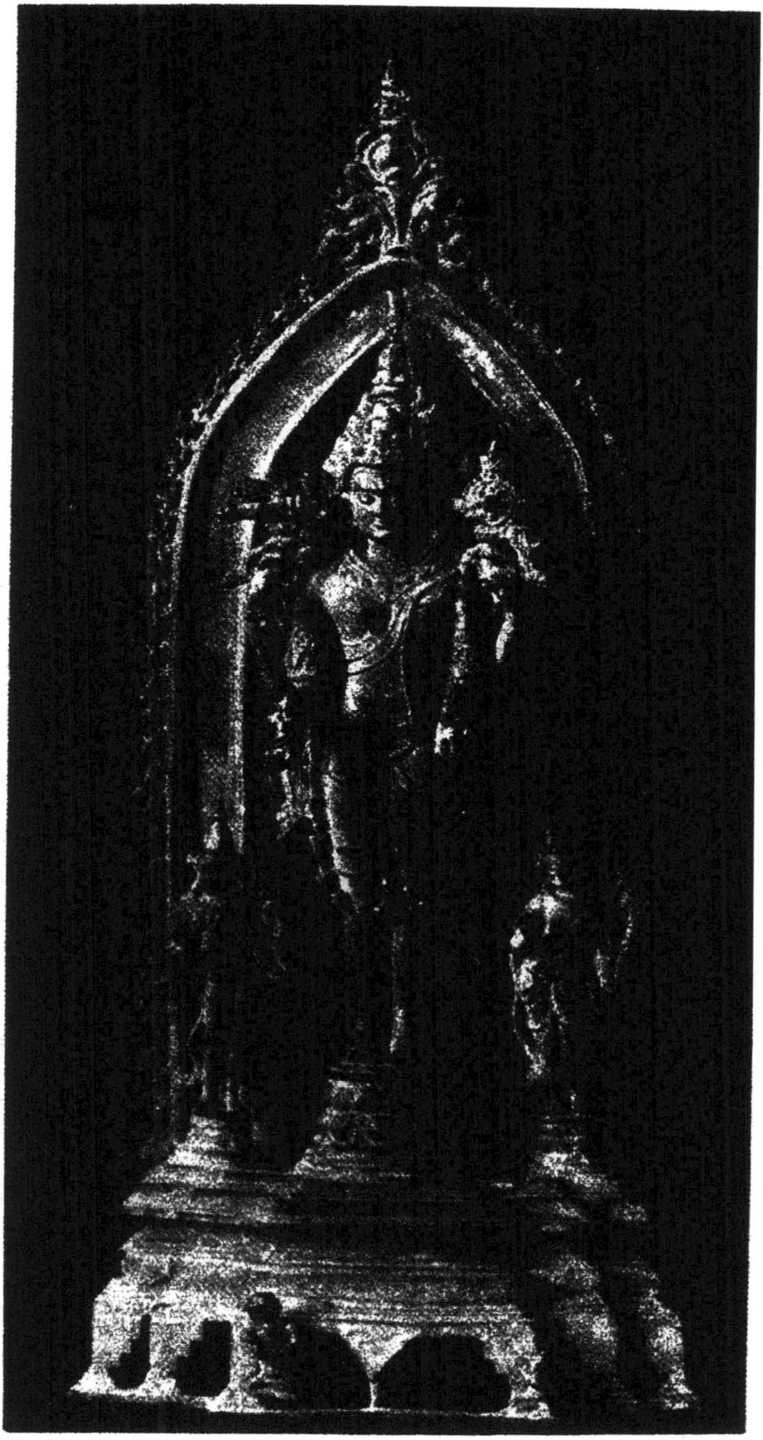

Fig. 32
Viṣṇu
11th century
Calcutta. Brass

Fig. 33. *(top)*. **Māra Dharṣaṇa (temptation of Buddha). From Borobuḍur, Java. Late 8th century.**

Fig. 34. *(bottom)*. **Army, gallery relief. From Angkor Wat, Cambodia. Middle 12th century.**

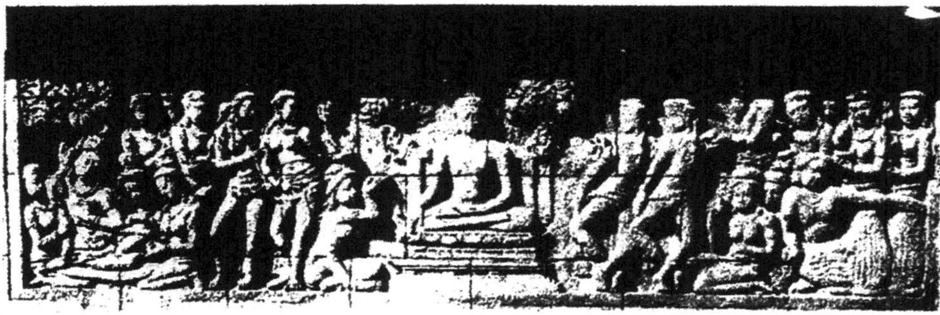

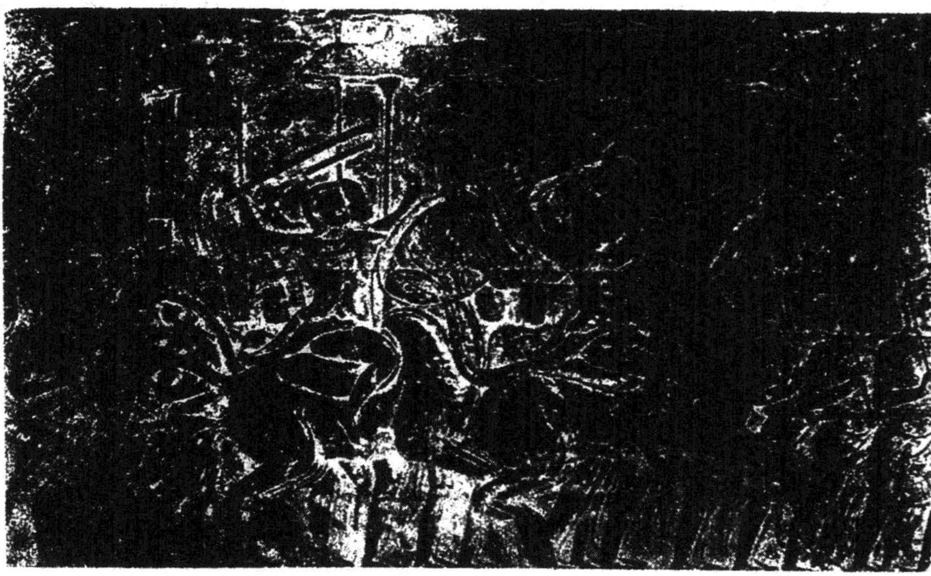

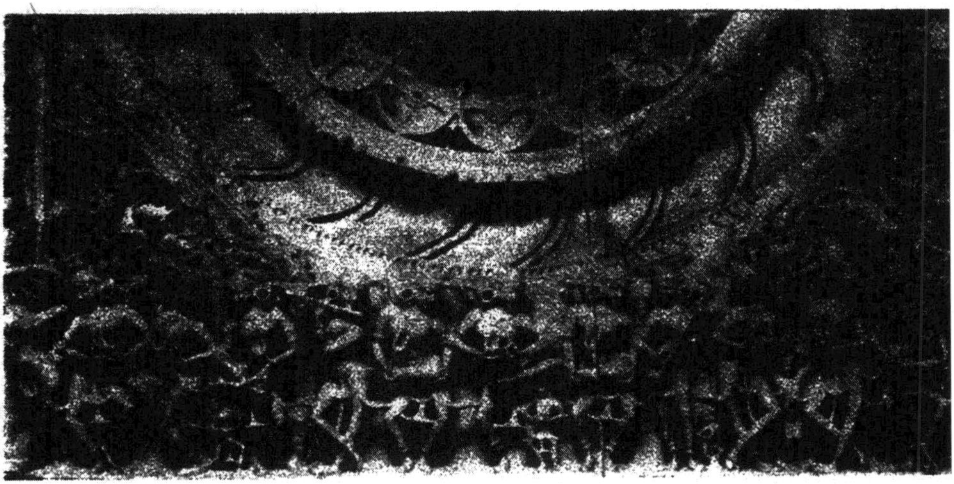

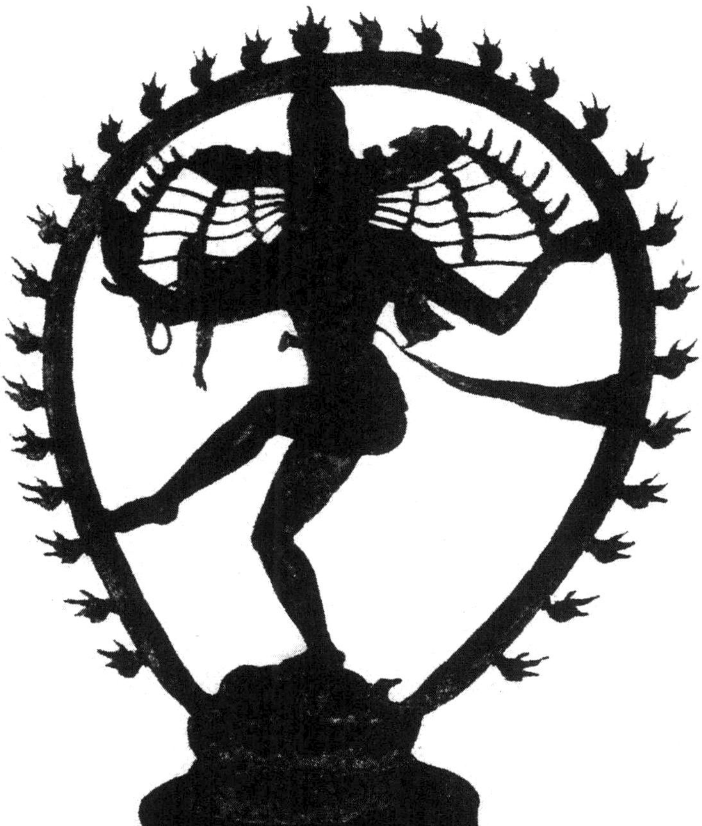

Fig. 35. *(top)*
Frieze of dancers
From Dilwārā
(Mt. Ābu)
10th century. Marble

Fig. 36. *(left)*
Śiva as Naṭarāja
16th century
Copper
Madras Museum

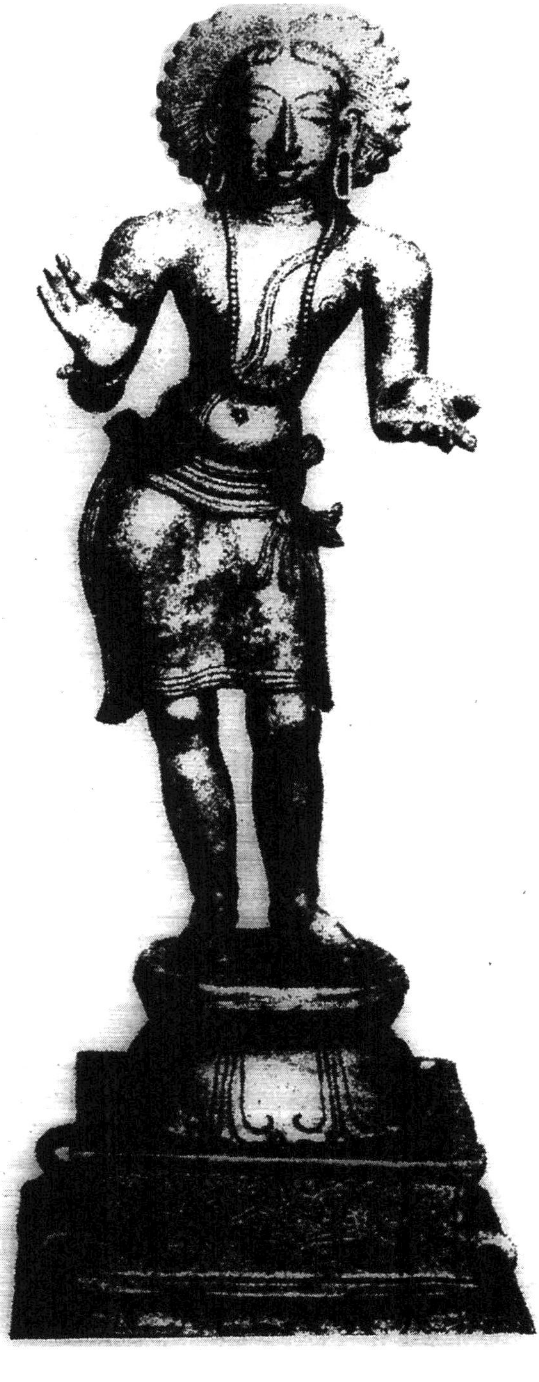

Fig. 37. Māṇikka Vāsagar
From Polonnāruva, Ceylon
13th century. Copper

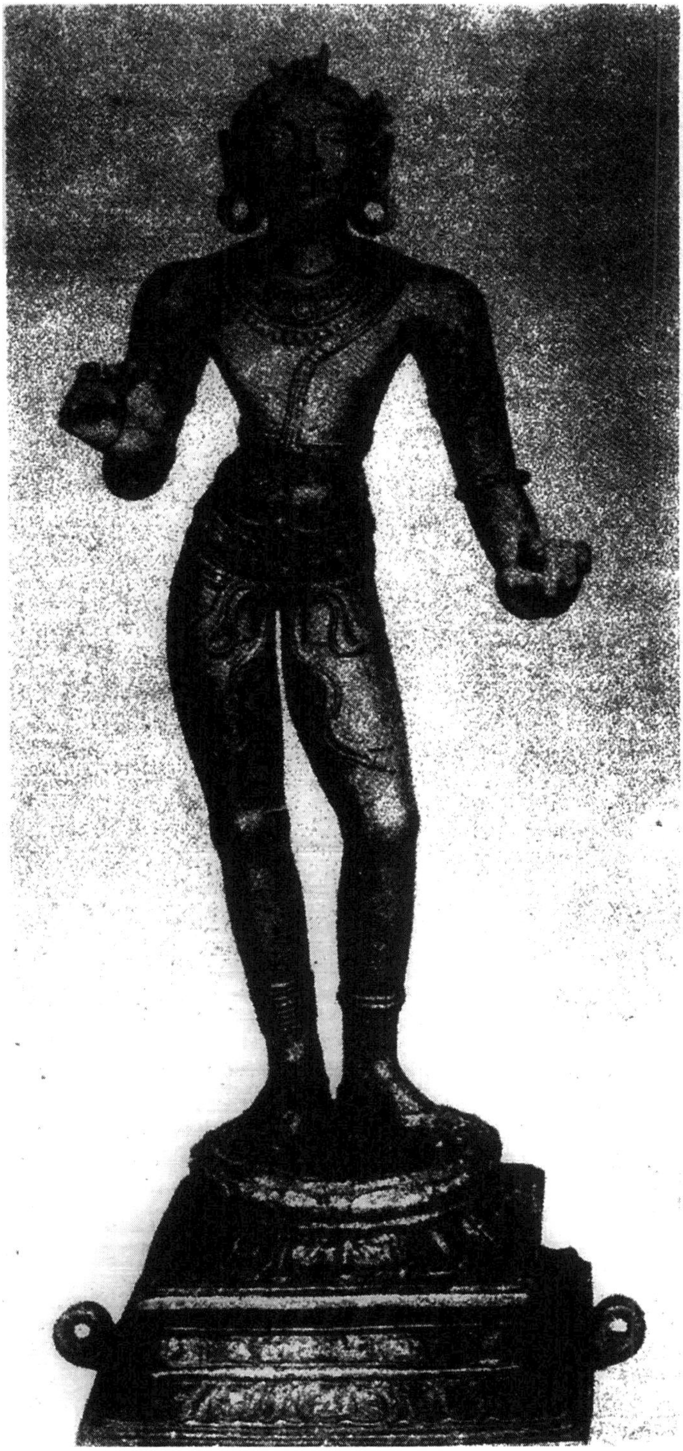

Fig. 38. Sundara Mūrti
From Polonnāruva, Ceylon
13th century. Copper

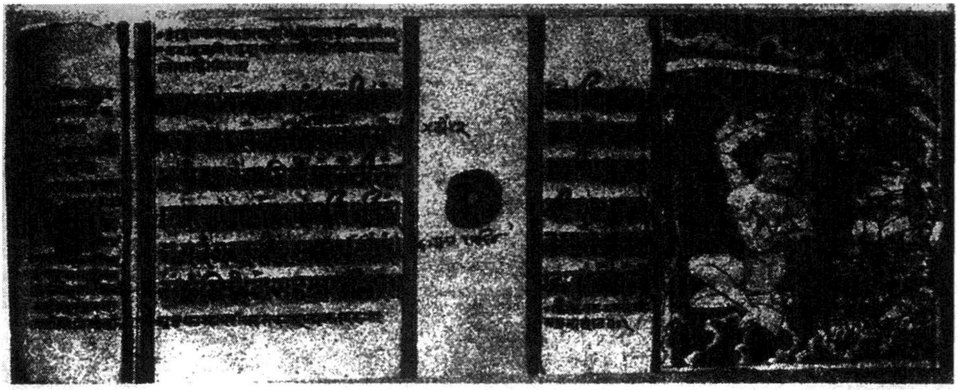

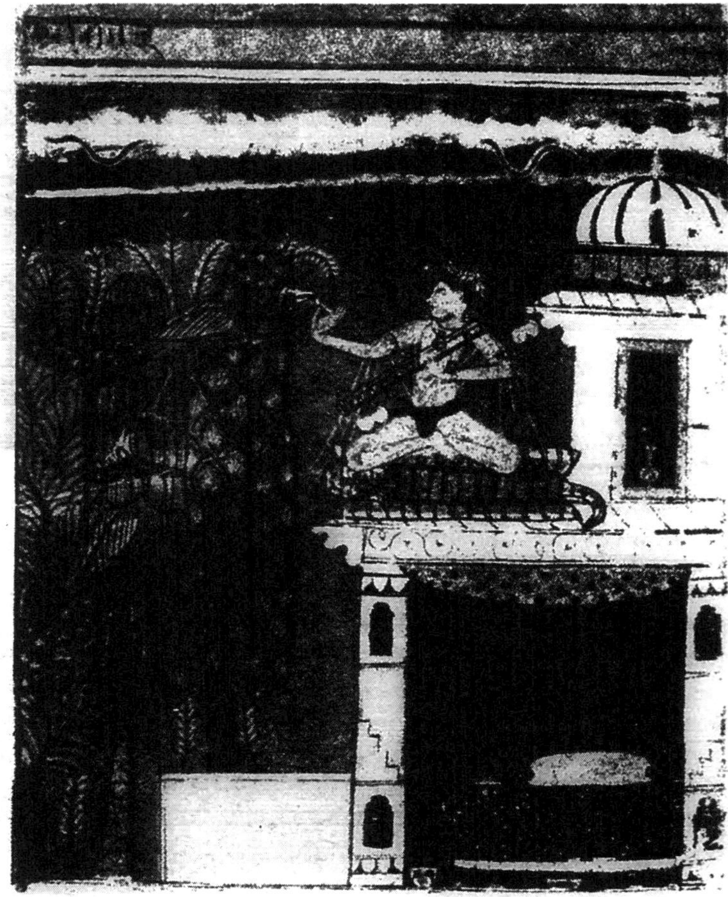

Fig. 39 *(top)*
Dīkṣā of Mahāvīra
Kalpasūtra Ms.
From Gujarat
About 15th century
Paper

Fig. 40. *(right)*
Śrī Rāgiṇī
Late 16th century
Rajput, Rājasthānī
Paper

Fig. 41. Madhu-mādhavī Rāgiṇī. Early 17th century. Rajput, Rājasthānī. Paper

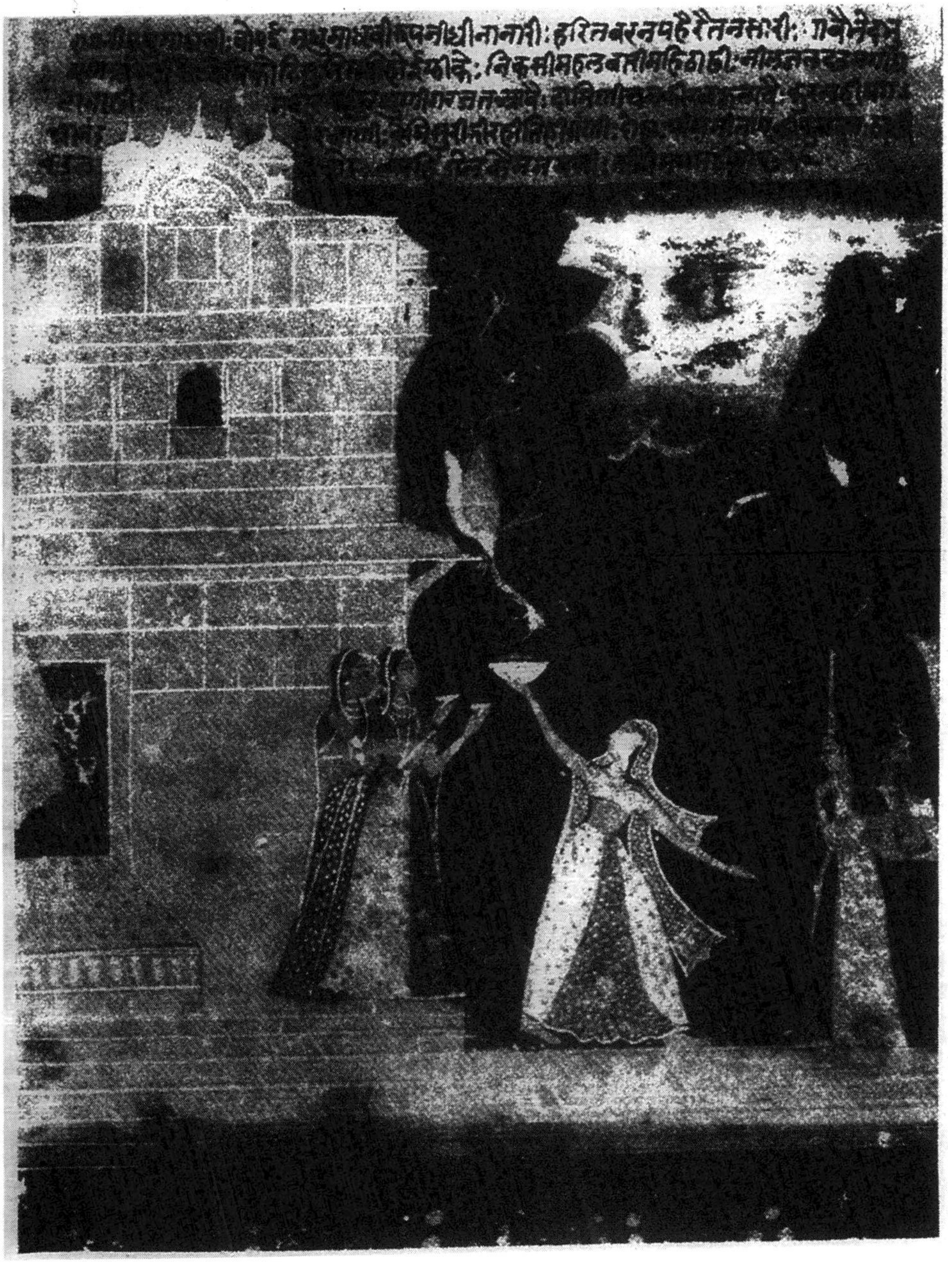

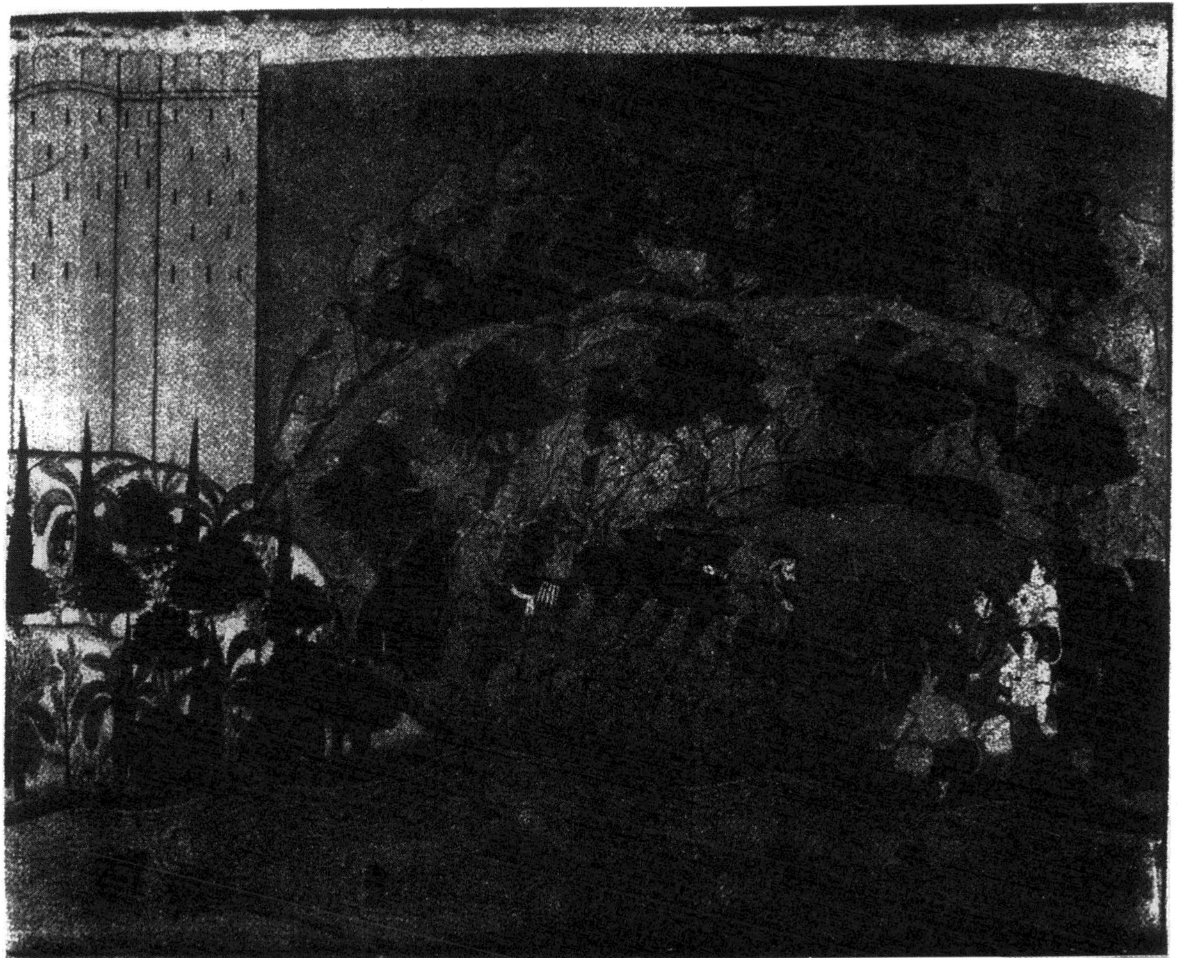

Fig. 42 *(left)*
Siege of Laṅkā
(Rāmāyaṇa)
Rajput, Pahāṛī
Late 17th century
Paper

Fig. 43. *(bottom)*
Rāmāyaṇa
(Vana-parva)
ca. **1700 (?). Paper**

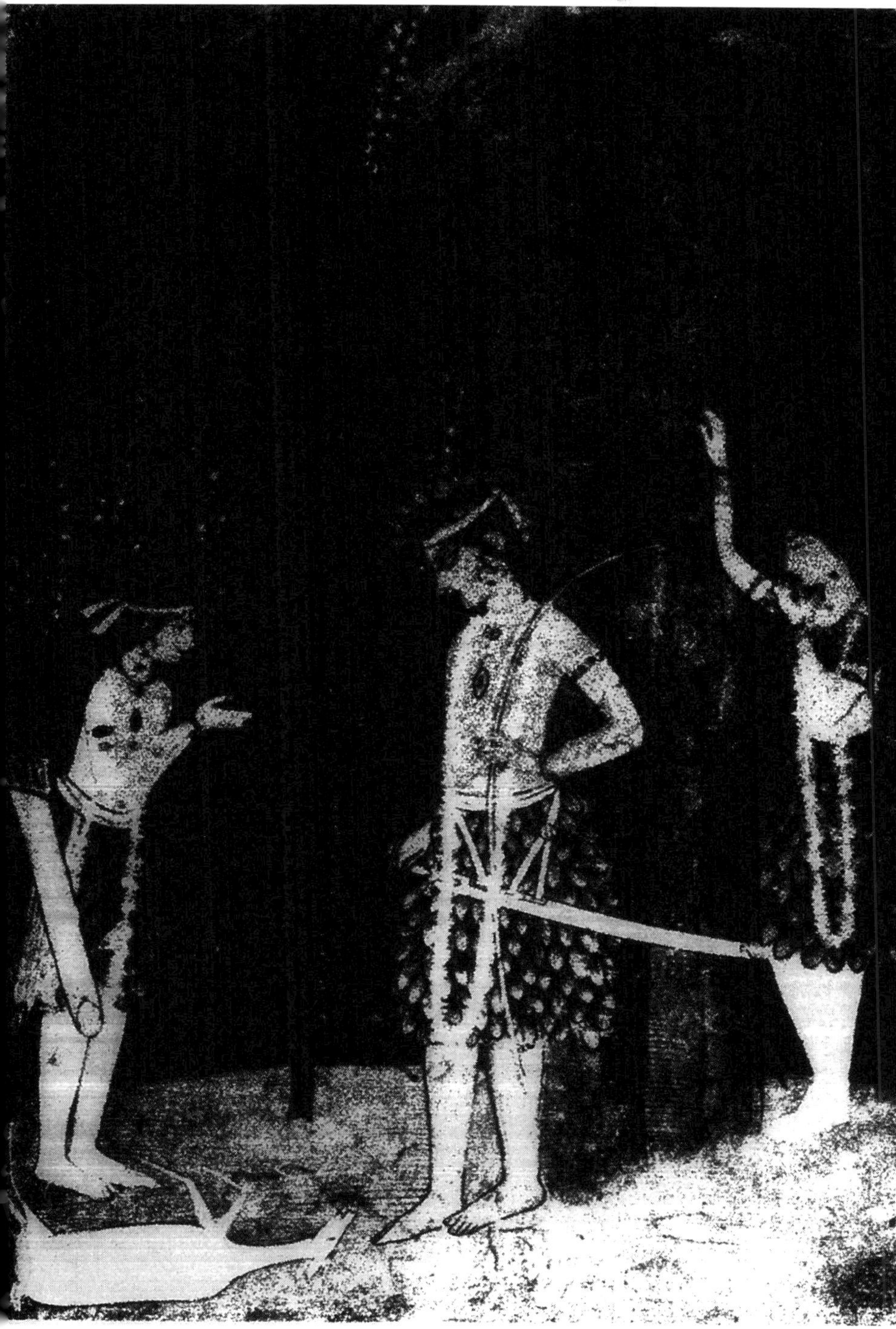

Fig. 44. Kṛṣṇa Veṇugopāla. *ca.* 1700 (?). Pape

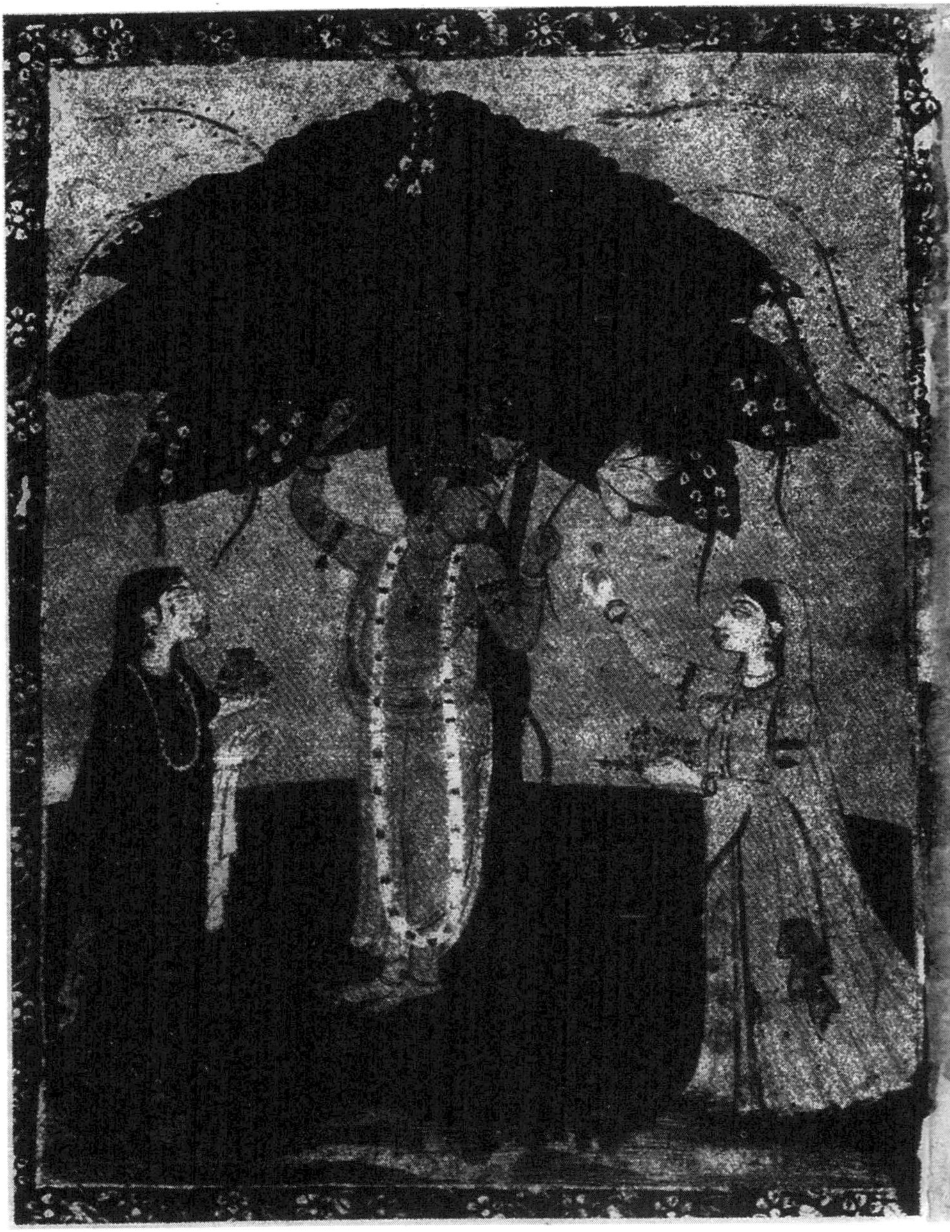